COMPACT *Research*

Teenage Sex and Pregnancy

Peggy J. Parks

Teenage Problems

ReferencePoint
Press®

San Diego, CA

© 2012 ReferencePoint Press, Inc.
Printed in the United States

For more information, contact:
ReferencePoint Press, Inc.
PO Box 27779
San Diego, CA 92198
www.ReferencePointPress.com

Picture credits:
Cover: iStockphoto.com and Thinkstock/Comstock
Maury Aaseng: 31–33, 45–47, 59–61, 74–76
Landov: 17
Dr. P. Marazzi: 12

LIBRARY OF CONGRESS CATALOGING-IN-PUBLICATION DATA

Parks, Peggy J., 1951–
    Teenage sex and pregnancy / by Peggy J. Parks.
        p. cm. — (Compact research series)
    Includes bibliographical references and index.
    ISBN-13: 978-1-60152-168-2 (hardback)
    ISBN-10: 1-60152-168-5 (hardback)
    1. Teenagers—Sexual behavior—Juvenile literature. 2. Teenage pregnancy—Juvenile literature. 3. Sex instruction for children. I. Title.
    HQ27.P36   2012
    306.874'3—dc22
                                                        2011012468

Contents

Foreword

As modern civilization continues to evolve, its ability to create, store, distribute, and access information expands exponentially. The explosion of information from all media continues to increase at a phenomenal rate. By 2020 some experts predict the worldwide information base will double every 73 days. While access to diverse sources of information and perspectives is paramount to any democratic society, information alone cannot help people gain knowledge and understanding. Information must be organized and presented clearly and succinctly in order to be understood. The challenge in the digital age becomes not the creation of information, but how best to sort, organize, enhance, and present information.

ReferencePoint Press developed the *Compact Research* series with this challenge of the information age in mind. More than any other subject area today, researching current issues can yield vast, diverse, and unqualified information that can be intimidating and overwhelming for even the most advanced and motivated researcher. The *Compact Research* series offers a compact, relevant, intelligent, and conveniently organized collection of information covering a variety of current topics ranging from illegal immigration and deforestation to diseases such as anorexia and meningitis.

The series focuses on three types of information: objective single-author narratives, opinion-based primary source quotations, and facts and statistics. The clearly written objective narratives provide context and reliable background information. Primary source quotes are carefully selected and cited, exposing the reader to differing points of view. And facts and statistics sections aid the reader in evaluating perspectives. Presenting these key types of information creates a richer, more balanced learning experience.

For better understanding and convenience, the series enhances information by organizing it into narrower topics and adding design features that make it easy for a reader to identify desired content. For example, in *Compact Research: Illegal Immigration*, a chapter covering the economic impact of illegal immigration has an objective narrative explaining the various ways the economy is impacted, a balanced section of numerous primary source quotes on the topic, followed by facts and full-color illustrations to encourage evaluation of contrasting perspectives.

The ancient Roman philosopher Lucius Annaeus Seneca wrote, "It is quality rather than quantity that matters." More than just a collection of content, the *Compact Research* series is simply committed to creating, finding, organizing, and presenting the most relevant and appropriate amount of information on a current topic in a user-friendly style that invites, intrigues, and fosters understanding.

Teenage Sex and Pregnancy at a Glance

Sex Among Teens

A youth risk study published in 2010 by the Centers for Disease Control and Prevention (CDC) showed that 46 percent of teenagers have had sex at some point in their lives, and 34 percent are currently sexually active.

Declining Teen Sex

The CDC reports that since 1991 the number of teenagers who have ever had sex has declined, as has the number of teens who are currently sexually active.

Teen Pregnancy

A 2010 report by the Guttmacher Institute showed that teen pregnancies totaled 742,990 in 2006, which is a decrease from nearly 1.2 million in 1980.

International Comparisons

The United States has the highest teen pregnancy and birth rate of all industrialized countries.

Sexually Transmitted Diseases

Nearly half of all new cases of STDs reported to the CDC are among teenagers and young adults aged 15 to 24.

Influences

Studies have shown that the strongest influences on teen attitudes about sex are parents, religious faith, friends, and the media.

Risks to Babies

Babies born to teenage mothers have a high risk of being born prematurely and with low birth weight. Child neglect and abuse are also more common in teen-parented families.

Sex Education

What to teach teenagers about sex is controversial. Some believe they should only be taught to abstain from sex, while others argue that teens should also be given information about sex and contraception.

Overview

❝Teen sexual activity is costly, not just for teens, but also for society. Teens who engage in sexual activity risk a host of negative outcomes including STD infection, emotional and psychological harm, and out-of-wedlock childbearing.❞

Christine C. Kim and Robert Rector, research analysts with the Heritage Foundation.

❝Our philosophy is that sex is a normal, natural part of human relationships, even for teens—provided it's in the context of a healthy relationship, in which both parties are equally respected, have equal expectations, and are supportive and mindful of each other's feelings.❞

Maureen E. Lyon, a clinical psychologist, and Christina Breda Antoniades, a health writer, are coauthors of the book *My Teen Has Had Sex: Now What Do I Do?*

When Rachel Coleman thinks about her early teenage years, she remembers a fun, carefree time. She often made plans on the spur of the moment, whether it involved going to the movies, grabbing something to eat, or just hanging out with friends. "I guess I was pretty much your average teen,"[1] she says. During the summer before her senior year, Coleman began dating a boy whom she knew from high school. Before long they started having sex and did not always use a condom—which was a choice that would drastically change their lives.

One day after school started, Coleman became dizzy and passed out in the hallway. Assuming she was just weak from not eating breakfast that morning, she did not give the incident much thought. So, finding out that she was pregnant was a shock, as she explains: "It definitely was not a planned pregnancy and while being sexually active in our relationship, we could have been a lot safer, but we were not."[2] Coleman decided to go ahead with the pregnancy and had a baby boy in 2009. Although she loves her son dearly, she stresses that teenage girls need to be aware of the risks involved before they become sexually active: "If you are not at the point in your life where you are ready to give up your wants and needs for a baby, then you need to do everything to be as safe as possible if you still choose to have sex."[3]

Is Teenage Sex and Pregnancy a Serious Problem?

In June 2010 the Centers for Disease Control and Prevention (CDC) published the findings of a survey on the health-risk behaviors of high school students. The study involved more than 16,500 teenagers throughout the United States and included a number of questions about sexual activity. When asked if they had ever had sexual intercourse, 46 percent said yes, and slightly more than one-third said they were sexually active, meaning they had had sex during the previous three months. Whether this high frequency of teen sex is a *problem* is subjective. Many people consider teenagers too young and immature to engage in sexual relations, while others view sexual activity during the teen years as normal and natural. But as Coleman's experience shows, having sex poses serious risks, including unplanned pregnancy.

> " The CDC youth study showed a slight reduction in the number of sexually active teenagers during the past two decades, from 37.5 percent in 1991 to 34 percent in 2009. "

Despite the high percentage of teens who engage in sexual activity, teen attitudes on this issue appear to be changing. The CDC youth study showed a slight reduction in the number of sexually active teenagers during the past two decades, from 37.5 percent in 1991 to 34 percent in 2009. Over that same period of time, teen pregnancies have also declined. According to a January 2010 report by the research and policy organization the Guttmacher Institute, pregnancies among 15- to 19-year-old females in the United States totaled 969,280 in 1991. By 2006 the number had dropped to 742,990, which represents a 30 percent decline in teen pregnancies over the 15-year period.

Race and Ethnicity

Surveys have clearly shown that teenagers of all races and ethnicities are sexually active, although with some significant differences. According to the CDC youth study, the highest prevalence of sexual activity is found among black teenagers, with 50.3 percent of black males and 45 percent of black females saying they had had sex in the past three months. Hispanic males and females have the second highest prevalence, followed by white teens. The CDC also found that black teens were most likely to have multiple sexual partners, with nearly 29 percent saying they had had sex with four or more people, compared with 14.2 percent of Hispanic teens and 10.5 percent of white teens.

A particularly striking difference among these groups is the incidence of teen pregnancy, with birth rates for Hispanic and black teenage girls being more than twice as high as those of white teens. The reasons for this disparity are not well understood, although some studies suggest that acceptance of teen births is greater among the black and Hispanic communities than among whites. This is the perspective of Karole Lakota, who is a physician in a west Chicago neighborhood where the population is more than 90 percent black and Hispanic. A large part of Lakota's medical practice is working with young mothers, many of whom have second and third babies while they are teenagers. She explains: "I've seen some mothers almost applaud their teenage daughters when they find out [they're] pregnant. Others put their teen on birth control at their 12-year-old check-up and just assume their child is sexually active."[4]

International Comparisons

Although teen pregnancies are at the lowest rate they have ever been since such data have been tracked, the United States still has the highest teen pregnancy rate of all industrialized countries. According to a March 2011 CDC report, the number of US births among 15- to 19-year-old females was 39 per 1,000 in 2009. Comparatively, the United Kingdom has the highest teen birth rate in Western Europe—but with 24 births per 1,000 girls, it is still markedly lower than in the United States. The differences are even more pronounced when other European countries are included in the comparison. The US teen birth rate is more than 4 times higher than Germany, France, Norway, and Sweden; 6 times higher than Italy; and 9 times higher than the Netherlands.

> 66 **Although teen pregnancies are at the lowest they have ever been since such data has been tracked, the United States still has the highest teen pregnancy rate of all industrialized countries.** 99

Why such disparities exist is an issue of much speculation. Studies have produced no evidence that American teens are more sexually active than young people in European countries—in fact, many experts say that the opposite is true. Referring to teen sex in America versus Europe, Washington, DC, demographics specialist Carl Haub says, "There may be more sex there than here."[5] Some have theorized that girls in European countries have more abortions, but research does not support that. According to the group Advocates for Youth, the US teen abortion rate far exceeds that of Germany, France, the Netherlands, and most other developed nations.

A widespread belief about the global difference in teen pregnancy is that European teenagers are more consistent about using birth control than American teens are. Studies indicate, for example, that more than 80 percent of sexually active teen girls in Sweden, the Netherlands, and France regularly use contraception. This is in contrast to the United States; according to the CDC youth survey, 61 percent of teens use contraceptives.

The High Prevalence of STDs

Approximately 19 million new cases of sexually transmitted diseases (STDs) are reported to health officials each year—and nearly half are among teenagers and young adults. The authors of a November 2010 CDC study write: "Compared with older adults, sexually active adoles-

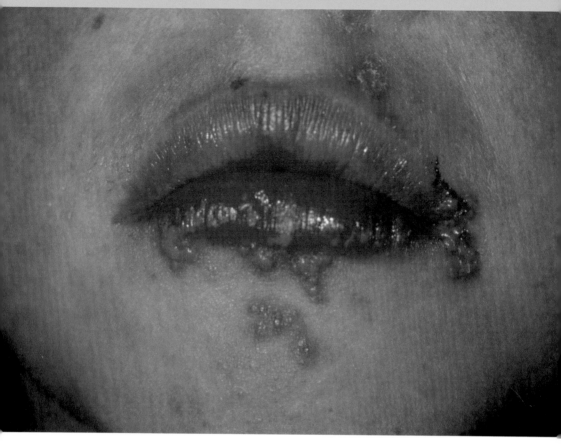

Sexually active teenagers risk contracting sexually transmitted diseases such as herpes. Although oral herpes (pictured) usually results from kissing someone who has an active infection around the mouth, genital herpes can be transmitted through sexual intercourse and oral sex.

cents aged 15–19 years and young adults aged 20–24 years are at higher risk of acquiring STDs for a combination of behavioral, biological, and cultural reasons."[6] The study analyzed STDs among all age groups from 2005 to 2009 and found that 15- to 19-year-old females had the highest rate of chlamydia and gonorrhea compared with all other age or gender groups. If not treated, both of these STDs can become serious enough to cause numerous health problems, including infertility.

Another finding of the study was that during 2008–2009, the highest increase of syphilis was in males and females aged 15 to 19. Although much less common among teenagers than in adults in their twenties and thirties, syphilis is one of the most dangerous STDs. Health risks range from sores and rashes on the skin during early stages, to organ damage and even death in more advanced stages.

The most prevalent STD, especially among teenagers and young adults, is the human papillomavirus (HPV). The American Cancer Society writes: "Some doctors think it is almost as common as the cold virus."[7] Scientists have identified more than 100 human papillomaviruses and have categorized them according to type, or strain. About 40 of these viruses are spread through sexual contact and can infect the genital areas, as well as the mouths and throats, of males and females. In many teens who are infected with HPV, the virus is destroyed by the immune system and disappears on its own. But HPV can pose serious health risks, causing problems that range from painful genital warts to several types of cancer.

What Influences Teenagers' Attitudes Toward Sex and Pregnancy?

Numerous factors have been shown to play a role in whether teens choose to have sex or to refrain from having sex. In teen-focused surveys, the most common influences cited include parents, morals and religious beliefs, friends, and the media. Yet which factors most influence teens is largely a matter of opinion, with studies producing results that can differ widely according to what organization performs the research and who the audience is.

This disparity was obvious in two reports that were published in 2010. One, by the National Campaign to Prevent Teen and Unplanned Pregnancy, found that 51 percent of 12- to 19-year-old girls were most influenced by their parents when making decisions about sex, compared with 20

> " **HPV can pose serious health risks, causing problems that range from painful genital warts to several types of cancer.** "

percent who said their friends were most influential. In sharp contrast was a survey conducted that same year by *Seventeen* magazine. When asked where they get advice about sex, 77 percent of the respondents said it was from their girlfriends. Their second most common source was the Internet, and the least common was information obtained from their mothers.

Although the extent of influence varies from study to study, the Internet and other types of media have been shown to have at least some impact on teenagers' attitudes toward sex and pregnancy. A growing number of parents, health officials, and teen pregnancy organizations are concerned about the effects of sexually explicit advertising and entertainment (including television, music, music videos, and the Internet) on teenagers. Adolescent medicine specialist Victor C. Strasburger says that the media "have arguably become one of the leading sex educators in the United States today."[8]

Disturbing Misconceptions

Despite the fact that nearly half of American teenagers have had sex, surveys have shown that many are either naive or lackadaisical about the risks involved with being sexually active. For a story published in the *Boston Globe* in December 2010, high school students from one Boston neighborhood shared their thoughts about sex. Some of their beliefs were surprisingly misguided, as the article's author writes: "Here are some things their friends think they know about sex: That you can't get pregnant if you have sex in water. That if you have oral sex, you won't get an STD. That there's no point in wearing a condom because it will probably break."[9]

> " Despite the fact that nearly half of American teenagers have had sex, surveys have shown that many are either naive or lackadaisical about the risks involved with being sexually active. "

The erroneous perceptions of many teenage boys were evident in a November 2009 survey titled *That's What He Said*. Among 15- to 18-year-old respondents, 43 percent were either unaware or did not believe that a girl could get pregnant during her period, 16 percent thought that pregnancy was not possible when a girl is taking birth control pills, and 19 percent were unaware that condoms are not foolproof. Yet despite these misconceptions, more than three-fourths of the teenage boys said they were *not at all confused* about how to prevent pregnancy. The study authors write:

"What they don't know about preventing pregnancy could get them into trouble, especially because they *think* they know it all."[10]

What Are the Consequences of Teenage Sex and Pregnancy?

Since surveys have revealed that teenagers often have erroneous beliefs about sexual activity, many are likely unaware of, or unconcerned about, the potential consequences. For example, studies indicate that numerous teens are careless about using condoms when they have sex. According to the CDC, condom use can prevent pregnancy in up to 98 percent of cases. Yet the agency's youth risk study found that 61 percent of teens who were sexually active had used a condom the last time they had sexual intercourse—meaning that 39 percent had not. Teen advocacy organizations say that a sexually active female who does not use contraceptives has a 90 percent chance of becoming pregnant within a year.

> **Those who think it would be nice to become teenage parents may have no idea that the odds are stacked heavily against them.**

Unfortunately, though, even when condoms are used faithfully they do not work 100 percent of the time. They may break during intercourse or fail because of defects in the material or use after the expiration date. Also, condoms cannot stop the spread of all STDs. Referring to sexually transmitted infections (STIs), clinical psychologist Maureen E. Lyon and health writer Christina Breda Antoniades explain: "All sexual contact carries some risk. Certain STIs (including herpes, syphilis, and HPV, to name three) can be transmitted even when a condom is used. . . . The bottom line: There's no such thing as risk-free sex."[11]

The Condom Controversy

One of the most controversial issues related to teen sex and pregnancy is whether schools should furnish young people with contraceptives. According to the CDC, an estimated 5 percent of high schools in the United States make condoms available to students. This became a topic of spirited debate in December 2009, when school officials in Milwaukee, Wisconsin, announced their intention to make condoms available in many of the city's high schools. The condoms would be available free of charge at schools that had a nurse on staff, but only when students requested them at the nurse's office. According to health curriculum specialist Brett Fuller, Milwaukee school officials still emphasize the importance of abstinence to students. "But," he says, "when they make the choice (to have sex) they need to have the tools and understanding on how to protect themselves from sexually transmitted infections and to prevent unwanted pregnancies."[12]

To gauge public opinion on this issue, the *Milwaukee Journal Sentinel* newspaper conducted an online survey shortly after the announcement was made by school officials. Nearly 8,000 people responded when asked whether Milwaukee Public Schools should make condoms available to students: 44 percent said yes and 56 percent said no.

Kids Having Kids

Surveys have shown that most teenage girls cringe at the thought of being pregnant, and boys often feel equally negative about getting a girl pregnant. But this perspective is not shared by all young people—some actually welcome the idea of having a baby. In a 2010 study by a team of CDC researchers, teen participants were asked, "If you got pregnant now/got a female pregnant now, how would you feel?" An average of 14 percent of teen girls and 18 percent of teen boys responded by saying that they would be either "a little pleased" or "very pleased." The researchers also heard profoundly different perspectives based on race and ethnicity. An average of 28.6 percent of Hispanic teens and 23.3 percent of black teens said they would either be "a little pleased" or "very pleased" to get pregnant or to cause a pregnancy, while fewer than 10 percent of the white teenagers felt that way.

Those who think it would be nice to become teenage parents may have no idea that the odds are stacked heavily against them. Lyon and Antoniades write: "Teens who express a desire to get pregnant likely haven't thought through the challenges or taken a hard look at the reality. They may also be focusing squarely on their own needs and desires without considering the needs of their future child."[13] Health officials stress that immense problems are associated with teenage pregnancy, such as

A young mother who became pregnant during her senior year in high school feeds her five-month-old daughter. Although teen sex and pregnancy are declining in the United States, the US teen pregnancy and birth rate is the highest in the industrialized world.

a high risk of having babies who are born prematurely, have low birth weight, and/or die during infancy. Studies have also shown that children of teenage parents are abused and/or neglected at a much higher rate than children born to older parents.

What Should Be Taught in Sex Education?

Of all the issues related to teenage sex and pregnancy, none is more controversial than whether sex education should focus solely on abstinence or take a more comprehensive approach, which emphasizes abstinence but also teaches how to prevent pregnancy and sexually transmitted diseases. Supporters of abstinence-centered programs acknowledge the high prevalence of sex among teenagers. But they contend that young people must be taught about the risks of having sex and learn that the only guaranteed way to avoid pregnancy and STD infection is to abstain from sex. The National Abstinence Education Association explains: "The focus of abstinence-centered education is to empower teens to avoid risk by making good health decisions, regardless of their sexual history, in contrast to so-called comprehensive sex education that sets the bar much lower, assuming teens will engage in high risk sexual behavior and focusing merely on reducing the risk of that behavior."[14]

> No matter where people stand on the sex education issue, most agree that teens would benefit from not having sex until they are older.

No matter where people stand on the sex education issue, most agree that teens would benefit from not having sex until they are older. Teens themselves stated this during the National Campaign to Prevent Teen and Unplanned Pregnancy's 2010 *With One Voice* survey. When asked if it was important for teens to be given a strong message about not having sex at least until they are out of high school, 87 percent said yes. Yet nearly half of the participants also said that teens should get information about both abstinence and contraception, which is a perspective that is shared by many health officials. Adolescent medicine specialist Margaret Blythe explains: "Comprehensive sexuality education *emphasizes* abstinence as the best option for adolescents, but also provides age-appropriate, medically accurate discussion and information for the prevention of sexually transmitted infections and unintended pregnancies."[15]

Because of the low rates of teen pregnancy and births in the Netherlands, many health officials praise the Dutch approach to sex education. Sexuality discussions are integrated into all levels of schooling, beginning at an early age. Kids are taught that sex is normal and natural, although they also learn the importance of being responsible when they have sex. Siebe Heutzepeter, who is the head teacher at a school in Amsterdam, shares his thoughts: "Here adults and children are better educated. It would be unthinkable for a Dutch parent to withdraw their child from sex education. . . . There is no point in telling children just to say 'no'—

this is a liberal country: you need to tell them why they are saying 'no' and when to say 'yes.'"[16]

A Challenging Issue

The statistics about teenage sex and pregnancy are disturbing to health officials. Each year an alarming number of teenagers become infected with STDs, and nearly 750,000 girls become pregnant. The good news, however, is that the prevalence of sex among American teenagers has declined over the years, as have teen pregnancies. This is a promising trend that will hopefully continue in the future.

Is Teenage Sex and Pregnancy a Serious Problem?

> 66The U.S. teen pregnancy and birth, sexually transmitted diseases (STDs), and abortion rates are substantially higher than those of other western industrialized nations.99

> Centers for Disease Control and Prevention, which seeks to promote health and quality of life by controlling disease, injury, and disability.

> 66Teens have sex whenever parents aren't around. Sex isn't just for the backseat of cars anymore.99

> Tom Clinton, a psychologist from Forest, Virginia, who is president of the American Association of Christian Counselors.

Every two years the Centers for Disease Control and Prevention conducts a comprehensive survey known as the *Youth Risk Behavior Surveillance*. The purpose is to evaluate health-risk behaviors that contribute to the leading causes of death, disability, and social problems among high school students in the United States. According to the 2008–2009 survey, which was published in June 2010, sexual activity among teens has declined since the 1990s. When asked if they have ever had sexual intercourse, 46 percent of teens said they had, which is considerably lower than the 59 percent reported in 1991. Two other areas that saw reductions in sexual activity were the number of teens who are currently sexually active, and the number who have been sexually involved with four or more partners.

Yet even with this decline, many health officials remain concerned about the high number of young people having sex. More than 700,000 girls become pregnant each year; the US teen birth rate is higher than in all other industrialized countries, and tens of thousands of young people have been infected by STDs. Sheila Overton, a physician from Los Angeles who specializes in obstetrics and gynecology, shares her thoughts: "Fewer teens are having sexual intercourse than they were in 1991, and fewer say they have had sexual intercourse with four or more persons. That's the good news. However, although teen sex has declined since 1991, we're still looking at a situation where *more than six in ten 12th grade high school students have had sexual intercourse.*"[17]

"Back on Track"

One year before the CDC released its report on declining sexual activity among teenagers, the agency made an announcement that shocked health care professionals and teen advocacy organizations. After decreasing every year since 1991, the US teen birth rate rose 3 percent from 2005 to 2006. The largest increase was among African American teens, whose birth rate jumped 5 percent over the one-year period. This was followed by a 4 percent increase for American Indian/Alaska Native teens, 3 percent for non-Hispanic white teens, and 2 percent for Hispanic teens. Upon hearing the news, the National Campaign for Teen and Unplanned Pregnancy's Bill Albert expressed his concern: "What you have is a serious, profound change in an issue where we had nothing but good news to report for almost two decades."[18]

Albert had no way of knowing that this "profound change" would be short-lived. Later reports by the CDC showed that while the teen

> " More than 700,000 girls become pregnant each year; the US teen birth rate is higher than in all other industrialized countries, and tens of thousands of young people have been infected by STDs. "

birth rate again rose slightly in 2007, it dropped 2 percent the following year. But an astounding discovery was made when researchers analyzed data from 2009. The teen birth rate had dropped 6 percent to 39.1 births per 1,000 teen girls—the lowest number since researchers began tracking such information in 1940. Upon learning of the sharp decline in teen births, advocacy groups were elated, which was apparent in a statement by the National Campaign's chief executive, Sarah Brown: "Just in time for the holidays, a steep decline in teen birth has been announced. We now are, thankfully, back on track."[19]

> **Although the majority of teenage girls who have sex do not become pregnant, research suggests that naïveté plays a major role among many who do.**

The 2010 CDC report revealed the teen birth rate for 2009 but not the number of teenage pregnancies for that year. This is because the number of births is taken directly from recorded birth certificates, while determining the pregnancy rate involves compiling the sum of live births, abortions, and miscarriages. Thus, the process is more complex and takes much longer to calculate. As of January 2010, the latest data available were from 2006, when there were 742,990 teen pregnancies. Even if a more recent total proves to be lower, health officials say that the high number of teenage girls becoming pregnant each year is a cause for serious concern.

Why So Many Pregnancies?

Although the majority of teenage girls who have sex do not become pregnant, research suggests that naïveté plays a major role among many who do. In a 2010 study by the National Campaign to Prevent Teen and Unplanned Pregnancy, 78 percent of the teen respondents said they had all the information they needed to avoid an unplanned pregnancy—yet half admitted that they knew little or nothing about condoms and how to use them. When asked the main reasons why they would have unprotected sex, 43 percent of the teens said they were willing to take the risk because they did not think anything would happen to them. Equally as troubling was that one-third of teens said the use of birth control was irrelevant because "when it is your time to get pregnant, it will happen."[20]

Many teenagers are well aware of the importance of using some form of contraception when they have sex, but not all of them use good judgment when choosing a method. One example is the high number of young people who attempt to prevent pregnancy by relying on the rhythm method, which involves abstaining from sex during the time of the month that a girl is ovulating. Since it is possible for girls to become pregnant at any time of the month, the rhythm method is an unreliable type of birth control. Despite the risk, however, the practice appears to be growing among teens. According to a June 2010 study by CDC researchers, 17 percent of teenage girls used the rhythm method from 2006 to 2008, which is an increase of 6 percentage points over 2002 when 11 percent said they had relied on it. This trend is profoundly disturbing to health officials because of the potential for increased teen pregnancies.

> " Not only does Mississippi have the highest number of teen births, it leads the country in all areas of teen sexual activity. "

Yet even young people who are knowledgeable about contraceptives, and are diligent about using them, can be faced with an unexpected pregnancy. This was the case with Patrick Potter, a teenager from the northeastern part of England. Potter and his girlfriend had been together for about a year when they found out she was pregnant. He writes: "She was still at school, and was on the pill, so we were shocked. Abortion was out of the question—neither of us believe in it. But I was frightened."[21]

A Troubled State

Studies have clearly shown that teenagers in all 50 US states are sexually active, but in some states the teen sex and pregnancy problem is much worse than in others. According to an October 2010 report by the CDC, Mississippi has the highest teen birth rate in the United States. With 65.7 births per 1,000 teenage girls, the state's rate is 58 percent higher than the national average. New Mexico, which formerly led the country in teenage births, now holds second place, followed by Texas, Arkansas, and Oklahoma (in that order).

Not only does Mississippi have the highest number of teen births, it leads the country in all areas of teen sexual activity. For instance, the CDC youth risk survey found that 61 percent of Mississippi teens have had sexual intercourse, compared with the national average of 46 percent. Mississippi also had the highest number of teens who had their first sexual encounter before the age of 13, the number who had sex with four or more partners, and the number who were currently sexually active.

Numerous theories have been posited about why Mississippi has this problem with teen sex and pregnancy, but substantive data are rare. Many are convinced that it is due to the prevailing belief in the state that parents, rather than schools, should teach kids about sex. According to a November 17, 2010, story in a Jackson, Mississippi, newspaper, school districts that do offer sex education typically follow the state Department of Education's guidelines, which call for basic education about STDs and AIDS and focus the teaching solely on sexual abstinence until marriage. As the article states: "School districts can teach comprehensive sex education if a local school board votes and adopts such a policy. But without public support—or legislation requiring school districts to adopt a specific policy—most school districts have not taken up the issue."[22]

A study published in September 2009 found a connection between high rates of teen pregnancy and states such as Mississippi, whose residents embrace conservative religious beliefs. According to the researchers who performed the study, this could be because the most conservative religions follow a literal interpretation of the Bible, and therefore may frown on the use of contraception. If teens subscribe to that belief and are not also taught about the potential consequences of having sex, teenage pregnancies will inevitably rise. Joseph Strayhorn, who is with Drexel University College of Medicine and the University of Pittsburgh, explains: "Religious communities in the U.S. are more successful in discouraging the use of contraception among their teenagers than they are in discouraging sexual intercourse itself."[23]

The Growing Prevalence of Oral Sex

A great deal of media attention has been devoted to the perceived increase in oral sex among teenagers. But research devoted to this issue is uncommon, as developmental psychologist Bonnie Halpern-Felsher explains: "Most studies on adolescent sex have focused on vaginal sex, thus leaving important questions concerning adolescents' attitudes, perceptions, and experiences with oral sex untapped."[24] Halpern-Felsher was involved in a study of 637 high school students who completed surveys about their sexual behaviors every six months over a three-year period. The researchers' goals were to evaluate teenagers' beliefs about oral sex versus vaginal sex, the relationship (if any) between oral and vaginal sex, and the positive or negative outcomes experienced by teens who had engaged in oral sex, vaginal sex, or both.

The study, which was published in March 2011, produced several important findings, one of which was that oral sex was more prevalent among teens than vaginal sex. "Teens don't consider oral sex to be sex," says Halpern-Felsher, "and many are not aware of the risks involved."[25] The researchers also found that oral sex was a "gateway" to sexual intercourse, with many teens who engage in oral sex for the first time going on to have vaginal sex within six months. This was especially true of the youngest teens. Of those who had engaged in oral sex by the ninth grade, only 9 percent did not go on to have sexual intercourse by the eleventh grade. Halpern-Felsher shares her thoughts: "We need to make sure teens know that if they do choose to have oral sex, certainly it does involve less risk than intercourse, but it's not risk-free."[26]

> **Because of the risks involved with oral sex, health officials are concerned about its growing prevalence among teenagers.**

Because of the risks involved with oral sex, health officials are concerned about its growing prevalence among teenagers. Some STDs (such as HPV, herpes, syphilis, and gonorrhea) can be spread through oral sex with an infected partner. HPV, for instance, has been associated with cancers of the mouth and throat, and teens who engage in oral sex have an increased risk of developing cancer later in life. This has long been an issue of concern for Maura Gillison, a physician at Ohio State University who studies the link between HPV and cancers of the head and neck. Gillison refers to one study that found an eightfold risk of mouth and throat cancer among people who had performed oral sex on six or more partners compared with those who had never engaged in oral sex. This is crucial for teens to know because, according to the Oral Cancer Foundation, oral cancers connected with HPV occur most frequently among young people.

Not to Be Taken Lightly

Even though sexual activity among teenagers has declined over the years, health officials emphasize that teen sex and pregnancy remains a serious problem. Studies have shown that many teens are naive about the possible risks of being sexually involved or are unconcerned because they think nothing will happen to them. Nearly 40 percent of young people have said that they engage in unprotected sex, while numerous teens use unreliable methods of birth control such as the rhythm method. Despite the fact that oral sex poses substantial health risks, its prevalence is growing among teenagers, who mistakenly believe that it is risk free. So what, if anything, can be done to address these problems? Unfortunately, no one can answer that question with any certainty.

Primary Source Quotes*

Is Teenage Sex and Pregnancy a Serious Problem?

Primary Source Quotes

66 Many older teens admit that there is a good chance they will have unprotected sex in the next few months even though the vast majority say they do not want to get pregnant or cause a pregnancy. 99

Katherine Suellentrop, "The Odyssey Years: Preventing Teen Pregnancy Among Older Teens," National Campaign to Prevent Teen and Unplanned Pregnancy, September 2010. www.thenationalcampaign.org.

Suellentrop is assistant director of research for the National Campaign to Prevent Teen and Unplanned Pregnancy.

66 Why do we always focus on the problem, whether it's adolescent pregnancy or diseases and so forth? Why aren't we talking about total life development, behavior and relationships? 99

Sarah Brown, "Are We Taking the Pleasure Out of Sex? What a Comprehensive Sexuality Program Should Look Like," *Conscience*, Spring 2009.

Brown is CEO of the National Campaign to Prevent Teen and Unplanned Pregnancy.

* Editor's Note: While the definition of a primary source can be narrowly or broadly defined, for the purposes of Compact Research, a primary source consists of: 1) results of original research presented by an organization or researcher; 2) eyewitness accounts of events, personal experience, or work experience; 3) first-person editorials offering pundits' opinions; 4) government officials presenting political plans and/or policies; 5) representatives of organizations presenting testimony or policy.

66 **Teenage birth rates have historically been higher for non-Hispanic black and Hispanic teenagers than for non-Hispanic white teenagers.** 99

T.J. Mathews, Paul D. Sutton, Brady E. Hamilton, and Stephanie J. Ventura, "State Disparities in Teenage Birth Rates in the United States," *NCHS Data Brief*, October 2010. www.cdc.gov.

Mathews, Sutton, Hamilton, and Ventura are with the Centers for Disease Control and Prevention's National Center for Health Statistics.

66 **The current decade can fairly be characterized as running in place—there has been essentially no change in the proportion of teens who have had sex since 2001, and condom use among sexually active teens seems to have stalled as well.** 99

National Campaign to Prevent Teen and Unplanned Pregnancy, "Fast Facts," June 2010. www.thenationalcampaign.org.

The National Campaign to Prevent Teen and Unplanned Pregnancy is dedicated to improving the lives of families and children by preventing teen pregnancy and unplanned pregnancy among single young adults.

66 **Of course, some teenagers have sex, and a fraction of those teens get pregnant. So do Missourians, Rastafarians, and people whose last names start with C.** 99

Mike A. Males, *Teenage Sex and Pregnancy: Modern Myths, Unsexy Realities*. Santa Barbara, CA: Praeger, 2010.

Males is a researcher with the Center on Juvenile and Criminal Justice in San Francisco.

66 **Clearly, teens having sex is risky behavior—and very young teens having sex is even more so.** 99

Sheila Overton, *Before It's Too Late*. Bloomington, IN: iUniverse, 2010.

Overton is a physician from Los Angeles who specializes in obstetrics and gynecology.

❝Few parents want to face the idea that their teens are having sex—but research shows that many teens are sexually active by high school, potentially putting themselves at risk of pregnancy and sexually transmitted infections.❞

Mayo Clinic, "Teens and Sex: Protecting Your Teen's Sexual Health," March 4, 2010. www.mayoclinic.com.

The Mayo Clinic is a world-renowned medical facility headquartered in Rochester, Minnesota.

❝For some parents, confronting an adolescent's sexuality triggers emotional struggles that have more to do with the parent's experience than the teen's.❞

Maureen E. Lyon and Christina Breda Antoniades, *My Teen Has Had Sex: Now What Do I Do?* Beverly, MA: Fair Winds, 2009.

Lyon is a clinical psychologist, and Antoniades is a health writer.

❝Misinformation and myths about sex and risks associated with teen sex abound and are especially rampant in the minds of fearful parents.❞

Evelyn Resh, *The Secret Lives of Teen Girls: What Your Mother Wouldn't Talk About but Your Daughter Needs to Know.* Carlsbad, CA: Hay House, 2009.

Resh is a certified nurse-midwife who specializes in the treatment of teenage girls.

Facts and Illustrations

Is Teenage Sex and Pregnancy a Serious Problem?

- According to the Guttmacher Institute, **70 percent** of male and female teens have had intercourse by their nineteenth birthday.

- In a 2008–2009 youth risk behavior survey by the Centers for Disease Control and Prevention, **14 percent** of high school students reported having four or more sexual partners.

- According to Advocates for Youth, among sexually experienced males, **73 percent** of American teens reported condom use the last time they had sex, compared with **88 percent** of French, **83 percent** of German, and **85 percent** of Dutch teens.

- Health officials in the United Kingdom report that there were **38,259** teen pregnancies in 2009 compared with **41,361** in 2008, which is a decline of **7.5 percent**.

- An October 2010 report by the Centers for Disease Control and Prevention showed that **Mississippi** has the highest rate of teen pregnancy in the United States (65.7 births per 1,000 teens) and **New Hampshire** has the lowest (19.8 births per 1,000 teens).

- According to Planned Parenthood's Rachael Phelps, even poor countries such as **Algeria, Sri Lanka, China,** and **Estonia** have lower teen birth rates than the United States.

Declining Teen Sexual Activity

According to data from the Centers for Disease Control and Prevention, the number of teens who had ever had sexual intercourse as of 2009 declined nearly 18 percent since 1991. Although percentages have varied through the years, statistics show a decrease in overall teen sexual activity between 1991 and 2009.

Percentage of teens who . . .

Had sexual intercourse
Were currently sexually active
Had sex with 4 or more partners

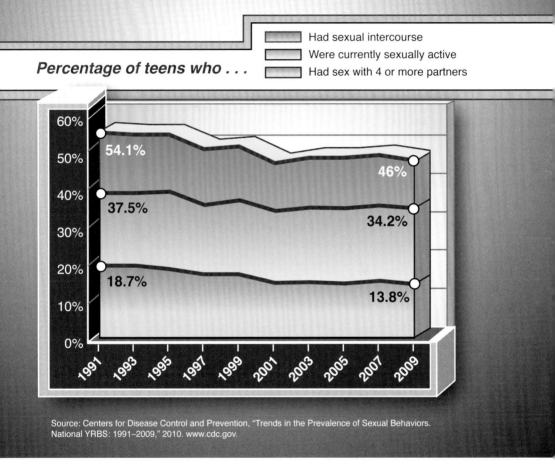

Source: Centers for Disease Control and Prevention, "Trends in the Prevalence of Sexual Behaviors. National YRBS: 1991–2009," 2010. www.cdc.gov.

- From 2007 to 2008 **Montana** was the only US state that reported a significant increase in the teen birth rate.

- In a survey of 1,000 adolescents that was published in February 2009, only **18 percent** of teen respondents agreed with the statement, "Having sexual intercourse would be a good thing to do at your age."

Many Teens Naive About Unprotected Sex

About 40 percent of sexually active teenagers admit that they do not use protection when they have sex. In a 2010 survey by the National Campaign to Prevent Teen and Unplanned Pregnancy, participants were asked why so many teens have unprotected sex, and their responses are shown on this chart.

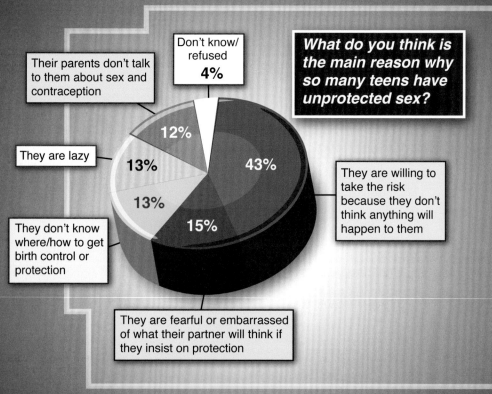

Their parents don't talk to them about sex and contraception

Don't know/ refused
4%

What do you think is the main reason why so many teens have unprotected sex?

They are lazy

12%

13%

13%

15%

43%

They are willing to take the risk because they don't think anything will happen to them

They don't know where/how to get birth control or protection

They are fearful or embarrassed of what their partner will think if they insist on protection

Source: Bill Albert, *With One Voice 2010: America's Adults and Teens Sound Off About Teen Pregnancy*, National Campaign to Prevent Teen and Unplanned Pregnancy, December 2010. www.thenationalcampaign.org.

- A survey published in the October 2010 issue of *Seventeen* magazine showed that **67.5 percent** of teen girls have had sex without a condom, and **60 percent** have had a pregnancy scare.

- Based on 2010 data from the United Kingdom's Office for National Statistics, **Britain** has the highest teenage pregnancy rate in Western Europe.

Sexual Activity Highest Among Black, Hispanic Teens

Studies show that teenagers of all races and ethnicities engage in sexual activity. But according to a youth risk survey by the Centers for Disease Control and Prevention, sexual activity is significantly more prevalent among black and Hispanic teens than among white teens.

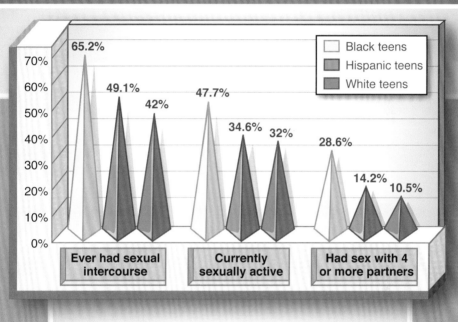

Source: Centers for Disease Control and Prevention, "Youth Risk Behavior Surveillance—United States, 2009," *Morbidity and Mortality Weekly Report*, June 4, 2010. www.cdc.gov.

- According to the advocacy group National Father Initiative, teenage fathers compose an estimated **30 percent** of the total incarcerated population, and at some prisons the number is closer to 60 or 70 percent.

- A 2009 youth risk behavior survey by the Centers for Disease Control and Prevention found that **7.4 percent** of high school students in the United States had been forced to have sexual intercourse.

What Influences Teenagers' Attitudes Toward Sex and Pregnancy?

❝Teens themselves say—are you sitting down?—parents influence their decisions about relationships and sex more often than peers, partners, or the popular media culture. Who knew?❞

Bill Albert, chief program officer of the National Campaign to Prevent Teen and Unplanned Pregnancy.

❝Today's young people face strong peer pressure to engage in risky behavior and must navigate media and popular culture that endorse and even glamorize permissiveness and casual sex.❞

Christine C. Kim and Robert Rector, research analysts with the Heritage Foundation.

When the MTV reality series *16 and Pregnant* debuted in June 2009, it attracted millions of viewers and quickly became one of the top-rated television programs. The premise of the show, according to the network, was to convey that teenage parents struggle with daunting challenges such as tumultuous relationships, financial problems, and stress related to school and work—in other words, being a teenage parent is anything but easy. As MTV's Tony DiSanto stated when the program was announced: "'16 & Pregnant' follows the journey of six young women going through an immensely life-changing experience at such a young age."[27]

After *16 and Pregnant* premiered, it was sharply criticized by those who believed it glamorized teen pregnancy. To find out how young people felt about that, a joint survey was conducted in 2010 by the National Campaign to Prevent Teen and Unplanned Pregnancy and Boys & Girls Clubs of America. Of the teenagers who said they had watched the show, only 15 percent thought it glamorized teen pregnancy, while 82 percent said that it had the opposite effect. When the teens were presented with the statement, "When a TV show or character I like deals with teen pregnancy, it makes me think more about my own risk (of becoming pregnant/causing a pregnancy) and how to avoid it,"[28] 67 percent of males and 79 percent of females agreed.

Sexuality and the Media

Still, however, a number of people remain unconvinced, believing that programs such as *16 and Pregnant* do put teen parenthood in a glamorous light. They are very concerned that these shows send the wrong message to young viewers, especially because the teens who are on the shows become famous. This, critics say, could potentially influence some young people to want to get pregnant themselves. Melissa Henson, who is with the Parents Television Council, explains: "Putting the stars of these reality shows on a magazine cover puts them on the same plane as any actress, singer, or other celebrity. It is sending the message to girls that if you get pregnant as a result of being sexually active, you could end up on TV or a magazine cover."[29]

The overall effect of the media on teenagers' attitudes about sex has long been an issue of concern for parents and health care professionals. Studies have shown that teens spend more than seven hours per day with a variety of different

> " **The overall effect of the media on teenagers' attitudes about sex has long been an issue of concern for parents and health care professionals.** "

media, with television being the most predominant. On behalf of the American Association of Pediatrics, Victor C. Strasburger published an article in August 2010 titled "Policy Statement—Sexuality, Contraception, and the Media." Strasburger writes that more than 75 percent of prime-time television programs contain sexual content, "yet only 14% of sexual incidents mention any risks or responsibilities of sexual activity. Talk about sex on TV can occur as often as 8 to 10 times per hour."[30]

Television is certainly not the only medium that bombards teenagers with sexual messages. Sex is also prominent in movies, radio programs, popular music, videogames, teen-focused magazines, and websites. Strasburger believes that sexually explicit media can influence teen ideas about becoming sexually active at an early age. Samantha Brea, a 17-year-old high school senior from Boston, shares that perspective, as she explains: "Media has a big impact in the way kids conduct themselves in sexual behaviors, and the influence they are getting isn't helping. You see videos and movies with people having multiple partners but they don't show the bad stuff about sex like getting STDs or unwanted pregnancies."[31]

> "Many teenagers say that they count on their parents to teach them what they need to know about sex."

Although sexual messages in the media have become more widespread—and more blatant—in recent years, CDC studies have shown a decline in sexual activity among American teenagers. These findings suggest that the media may not have the level of influence that some have claimed, as psychologist Laurence Steinberg and research scientist Kathryn C. Monahan write: "It is easy to point our collective finger at the entertainment industry, but it is likely that the most important influences on adolescents' sexual behavior may be closer to home than to Hollywood."[32]

The Double-Message Debate

A great deal of controversy exists over whether giving teens too much information about sex, such as telling them about contraception, can influence them to become sexually active. Lori Cole, who is executive director of the conservative lobby group Eagle Forum, explains: "We believe it's an inconsistent message. If you say, 'don't do it, it's not healthy for you, but if you're going to do it, do it this way,' that sends mixed signals to kids."[33] The National Campaign to Prevent Teen and Unplanned Pregnancy asked about this in its *With One Voice* survey. When asked to respond to the question, "Suppose a parent or other adult tells a teen the following: 'I strongly encourage you not to have sex. However, if you do, you should use birth control or protection.' Do you think this is a message that encourages teens to have sex?" nearly three-fourths of the teens said no.

Strasburger agrees that such a statement could send mixed signals—but he shares the perspective of those who say it does not encourage teens to have sex. He explains: "Telling teenagers, 'Wait until you're older to begin having sex, but if you can't wait, use birth control' is a double message. But it is a double message that every teenager in America can understand and benefit from."[34] Strasburger refers to Western Europe, where advertising that features contraceptives is prolifically targeted at teenagers. He writes: "Other countries advertise birth control products widely and have a much lower rate of teen pregnancy."[35]

The differences in advertising between Europe and the United States were illustrated in a slide show created by Rachael Phelps, a physician who works for Planned Parenthood in Rochester, New York. She refers to a "contrast in attitudes toward teen sexuality" and provides a number of examples to illustrate her point. One German magazine pictures a condom and an apple, and Phelps explains the connotation: "An apple and a condom a day keeps the STD away!"[36] Phelps adds that Germany's approach to safe sex, which is evident in the country's advertising, is based on research showing that honest, humorous messages about sex are effective because they influence teens in a positive way.

The Crucial Role of Parents

Many teenagers say that they count on their parents to teach them what they need to know about sex. In her book *Talking Sex with Your Kids*, author Amber Madison writes: "Many parents think that teens' friends most influence their decisions to have sex. But that's not the case. It's not their friends, the media, or even their partner that plays the biggest role in teens' sexual decision making. It's . . . their parents."[37] The fact that parents are often not aware of this was evident in a study published in the January 2011 issue of *Journal of Adolescent Health*. Nearly 98 percent of the parents surveyed indicated that they should be the primary source of sex-related information for their kids—but only 24 percent thought that this was actually happening. From this, the researchers concluded that parents often underestimate the importance of their role in educating young people about sex.

> **What is not so widely publicized is that religious faith and personal values are among the strongest influences on young people's attitudes about whether to become sexually involved.**

Even when parents do initiate discussions about sex, their kids do not always find the discussions beneficial. In the 2010 *With One Voice* survey, 80 percent of teens said it would be much easier to delay sexual activity and avoid teen pregnancy if they were able to have more open, honest conversations about these topics with their parents. When asked if they wished they could talk more freely about sex with their parents, 62 percent said that they did. Bill Albert writes: "Many parents understand that they should be talking to their children about relationships, love, sex, and contraception, but they freely admit that they don't know what to say, when to say it, or how to get the conversation started."[38]

Why Some Teens Say No

Innumerable articles have addressed the issue of teenage sex and pregnancy, and many discuss common influences on teens such as parents, teachers, friends, and the media. What is not so widely publicized is that religious faith and personal values are among the strongest influences on young people's attitudes about whether to become sexually involved. Los Angeles psychiatrist Miriam Grossman writes: "Sincere religious beliefs and practice in adolescence are inversely associated not only with teen sex, but with binge drinking, marijuana use, and cigarette smoking."[39]

The importance of religion was apparent in the report published in June 2010 by a team of CDC researchers. Teens were asked a number of questions about sexuality, and those who said they had never had sex were asked to explain why they made that decision. The most frequent reason stated (by 41.5 percent of teenage girls and 35 percent of teenage boys) was that having sex was against their religion or morals. This was given as the reason more than twice as often as the fear of pregnancy and over 5 times as often as the fear of STDs.

Studies by the National Campaign to Prevent Teen and Unplanned Pregnancy have also shown that teenagers' personal sense of right and wrong was a powerful influence in their decision whether to have sex. In the 2010 *With One Voice* survey, 73 percent of teens said they thought religious leaders and groups should be doing more to prevent teen pregnancy. Albert writes: "In short, many young people make decisions about sex based not just on what is safe but also on what they believe is right."[40]

Is the Brain to Blame?

One of the main concerns health care professionals have about teenagers becoming sexually involved is that young people do not always think about the potential consequences before having sex. Rather, they get lost in the moment and act impulsively, often regretting their actions later. Studies have shown that this may be influenced by biology because the brain is still developing during adolescence, so it functions differently from an adult brain. Grossman writes: "The area responsible for reasoning, suppression of impulses, and weighing the pros and cons of one's decisions is not fully developed. Furthermore, under conditions that are intense, novel, and stimulating, teens' decisions are more likely to be shortsighted and driven by emotion."[41]

Scientists have used magnetic resonance imaging (MRI) technology to study the human brain for years, and much has been learned about

> **The difference in the rate at which the various parts of adolescent brains develop is important to scientists as it could help explain why teenagers may engage in risky sexual practices—one part of the brain is seeking pleasure, while the area that should cause teens to stop and think first is still undeveloped.**

how it functions. According to the National Institute of Mental Health, by scanning a child's brain every two years as he or she grows up, researchers can clearly see the changes that take place as the brain matures. One finding is that the adolescent brain is hypersensitive to activities (such as sex) that trigger responses from dopamine, a chemical that helps control the brain's reward and pleasure centers. Among the last areas of the brain to develop is the frontal lobe, which is responsible for executive functions such as planning, impulse control, and reasoning.

The difference in the rate at which the various parts of adolescent brains develop is important to scientists as it could help explain why teenagers may engage in risky sexual practices—one part of the brain is seeking pleasure, while the area that should cause teens to stop and think first is still undeveloped. A December 16, 2010, *Newsweek* article explains: "The brains of a teen couple upstairs at a party, maybe a bit drunk, are firing like crazy in anticipation of sex; unfortunately, they're lacking full development of the brain regions that in an adult would interject with this urgent message: don't forget to use a condom."[42]

A Complex Combination of Factors

There are no easy answers to the question of what motivates some teenagers to become sexually active while others choose to abstain from sex. Studies have shown that parents play a crucial role in influencing teens' attitudes about sex, as do religious beliefs, friends, and the media. Yet even though these have all been shown to affect teens' attitudes about sex and their sexual behaviors, no one factor is solely responsible. Rather, a combination of factors is likely involved, as researchers from the University of Pennsylvania write: "Adolescents rely on multiple sources of information about sex, and no one source influences all types of beliefs associated with having sex."[43]

Primary Source Quotes*

What Influences Teenagers' Attitudes Toward Sex and Pregnancy?

66 **There is only one way to stop this [teen pregnancy] problem and that is to stop having sex. This sounds like an easy solution but peer pressure makes this choice almost impossible.** 99

Alexis Ware, "A Teenager's Thoughts: Pregnancy, Abortion, Sex and Peer Pressure, All Before Age 13!" Empowered Peace, September 27, 2010. www.empoweredpeace.org.

Ware is a senior at a high school where teen pregnancy is commonplace.

66 **Surveys often don't support the belief that peer pressure is the single most important culprit driving teens toward having sex.** 99

Sheila Overton, *Before It's Too Late*. Bloomington, IN: iUniverse, 2010.

Overton is a physician from Los Angeles who specializes in obstetrics and gynecology.

Bracketed quotes indicate conflicting positions.

* Editor's Note: While the definition of a primary source can be narrowly or broadly defined, for the purposes of Compact Research, a primary source consists of: 1) results of original research presented by an organization or researcher; 2) eyewitness accounts of events, personal experience, or work experience; 3) first-person editorials offering pundits' opinions; 4) government officials presenting political plans and/or policies; 5) representatives of organizations presenting testimony or policy.

Primary Source Quotes

❝Other significant sources of information on sexuality and influences on adolescent sexuality besides parents and the mass media include schools, political policy, and religious institutions.❞

Anne Bolin and Patricia Whelehan, *Human Sexuality: Biological, Psychological, and Cultural Perspectives.* New York: Routledge, 2009.

Bolin is a professor of anthropology at North Carolina's Elon University, and Whelehan is a professor of anthropology at the State University of New York at Potsdam.

❝Watching sex on TV increases the chances a teen will have sex, and may cause teens to start having sex at younger ages.❞

University of Michigan Health System, "Television and Children," YourChild Development & Behavior Resources, August 2010. www.med.umich.edu.

The University of Michigan Health System is a leading health care system and academic medical center located in Ann Arbor, Michigan.

❝We found no evidence that the initiation of sexual intercourse is hastened by exposure to sexy media.❞

Laurence Steinberg and Kathryn C. Monahan, "Adolescents' Exposure to Sexy Media Does Not Hasten the Initiation of Sexual Intercourse," *Developmental Psychology*, August 2, 2010. www.temple.edu.

Steinberg is a psychologist at Temple University, and Monahan is a research scientist at the University of Washington.

❝Teens overall consistently report that when it comes to their decisions about sex and contraception, their parents are a very important influence. This is true of older teens as well.❞

Katherine Suellentrop, "The Odyssey Years: Preventing Teen Pregnancy Among Older Teens," National Campaign to Prevent Teen and Unplanned Pregnancy, September 2010. www.thenationalcampaign.org.

Suellentrop is assistant director of research for the National Campaign to Prevent Teen and Unplanned Pregnancy.

"The impact of entertainment: the MTV reality show 'Teen Mom' is far more absorbing than the average sex-ed curriculum, and probably more influential as well."

Ross Douthat, "Sex Ed in Washington," *New York Times*, February 1, 2010.

Douthat is a conservative author and columnist for the *New York Times*.

"What about guilt? Guilt is a powerful variable; that is, if teens believe that teen sex is wrong, it does limit their behavior significantly."

Miriam Grossman, "You're Teaching My Child *What*? The Truth About Sex Education," Heritage Foundation, August 9, 2010. www.heritage.org.

Grossman is a psychiatrist from Los Angeles.

"Teens with strong religious beliefs are more likely to delay sex, as are teens whose parents talk to them about delaying sexual activity."

Maureen E. Lyon and Christina Breda Antoniades, *My Teen Has Had Sex: Now What Do I Do?* Beverly, MA: Fair Winds, 2009.

Lyon is a clinical psychologist, and Antoniades is a health writer.

"Fortunately, young people today have available a vast, largely unregulated Internet medium in which they can find information and communicate about sexual issues from a variety of standpoints."

Mike A. Males, *Teenage Sex and Pregnancy: Modern Myths, Unsexy Realities.* Santa Barbara, CA: Praeger, 2010.

Males is a researcher with the Center on Juvenile and Criminal Justice in San Francisco.

Facts and Illustrations

What Influences Teenagers' Attitudes Toward Sex and Pregnancy?

- In a 2010 survey by the National Campaign to Prevent Teen and Unplanned Pregnancy, **46 percent** of teenage participants said their parents most influenced their decisions about sex.

- Of the males aged 15 to 18 who participated in a November 2009 survey titled *That's What He Said*, **80 percent** agreed that there is too much pressure from society to have sex.

- Of teenage girls who participated in a survey published in the October 2010 issue of *Seventeen* magazine, **77 percent** said they got their sex advice from their girlfriends.

- A January 2011 study by the National Abstinence Education Association found that male adolescents gained information about sex from the **Internet, sex-related magazines,** and **books** significantly more often than teenage girls.

- A study published in January 2011 by the Guttmacher Institute found that most high school students were **wary of sexual health information on the Internet**, and when seeking such information they were much more likely to trust family members (usually parents), followed by educators, medical professionals, and friends.

Teens Say Parents, Friends Most Influential

In national surveys, teenagers have cited a number of factors that influence their thoughts and decisions about sex. According to a report published in December 2010 by the National Campaign to Prevent Teen and Unplanned Pregnancy, young people aged 12 to 19 are most influenced by their parents, with friends being the next most influential group.

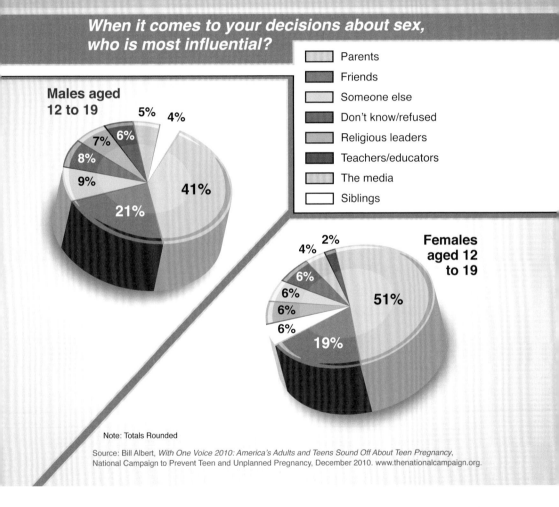

When it comes to your decisions about sex, who is most influential?

Legend:
- Parents
- Friends
- Someone else
- Don't know/refused
- Religious leaders
- Teachers/educators
- The media
- Siblings

Males aged 12 to 19: 41%, 21%, 9%, 8%, 7%, 6%, 5%, 4%

Females aged 12 to 19: 51%, 19%, 6%, 6%, 6%, 6%, 4%, 2%

Note: Totals Rounded

Source: Bill Albert, *With One Voice 2010: America's Adults and Teens Sound Off About Teen Pregnancy*, National Campaign to Prevent Teen and Unplanned Pregnancy, December 2010. www.thenationalcampaign.org.

- According to a 2010 study by the Centers for Disease Control and Prevention, more than **41 percent** of teen girls and **35 percent** of teen boys who did not have sex said it was because of their religion and/or morals.

Parents Underestimate Their Influence on Teens

A number of studies have shown that most teenagers count on their parents as a primary source of information about sex. According to a research paper published in January 2011, parents think they *should* provide this information to their teens—but as this graph shows, most believe that teens get most of their information on sexuality from friends and the media.

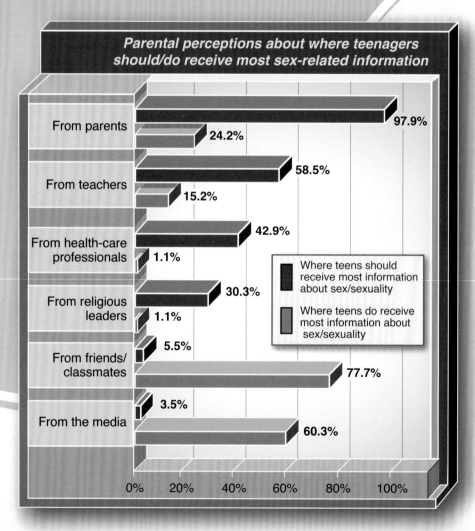

Parental perceptions about where teenagers should/do receive most sex-related information

From parents: 97.9% / 24.2%
From teachers: 58.5% / 15.2%
From health-care professionals: 42.9% / 1.1%
From religious leaders: 30.3% / 1.1%
From friends/classmates: 5.5% / 77.7%
From the media: 3.5% / 60.3%

Legend:
- Where teens should receive most information about sex/sexuality
- Where teens do receive most information about sex/sexuality

0% 20% 40% 60% 80% 100%

Note: Totals do not add up to 100 percent because participants were allowed to give multiple answers.

Source: Kathryn Allen Lagus et al., "Parental Perspectives on Sources of Sex Information for Young People," *Journal of Adolescent Health*, January 18, 2011. www.cfah.org.

Sexual Song Lyrics Linked to Teen Sex

Studies have shown that the media influence teens' thoughts and decisions about sexual behavior, although the extent to which this happens is often debated. To examine the potential effects of music on teens, a team of researchers conducted a study that focused on songs with lyrics that were sexually degrading, rather than portraying sex in a mutually respectful way. As this graph shows, the team found that the more teens were exposed to these types of song lyrics, the higher the likelihood of engaging in sexual intercourse.

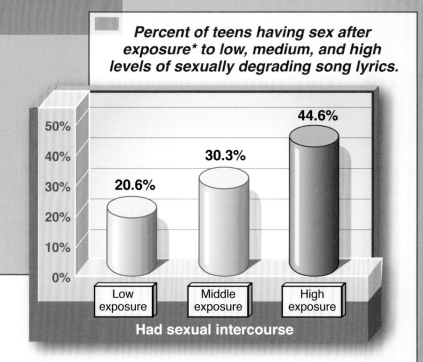

Percent of teens having sex after exposure* to low, medium, and high levels of sexually degrading song lyrics.

- Low exposure: 20.6%
- Middle exposure: 30.3%
- High exposure: 44.6%

Had sexual intercourse

*Exposure was calculated by multiplying each student's hours of music exposure by the percentage of his/her favorite artist's songs that contained sexually degrading lyrics.

Source: Brian A. Primack et al., "Exposure to Sexual Lyrics and Sexual Experience Among Urban Adolescents," *American Journal of Preventive Medicine*, April 2009. www.primack.net.

- In an Abt Associates survey of 1,000 adolescents that was published in February 2009, more than **50 percent** of teen respondents disagreed with the statement, "At your age right now, there is little your parents can do to keep you from engaging in sexual intercourse."

What Are the Consequences of Teenage Sex and Pregnancy?

❝The possibility of catching an STD or becoming pregnant doesn't seem real to many adolescents. If they worry about risk at all, they do so after having sex.❞

Mayo Clinic, a world-renowned medical facility headquartered in Rochester, Minnesota.

❝I couldn't believe it when Angela told me she was pregnant. We'd only been together a few weeks. I wasn't at all happy. I remember thinking, what will happen to the time I have with my friends? How will I cope?❞

Kenneth Pervis, a young man from the United Kingdom who was 18 years old when his girlfriend got pregnant.

With CDC studies showing that nearly 40 percent of teenagers do not use condoms, the implications are clear—for whatever reason, thousands of young people are putting themselves at risk for pregnancy and STD infection. When surveyed, many teens who are asked why they have not used condoms admit that they did not think about the consequences before having sex. This was the case with a teenager named Thomas. He and his girlfriend had sex, and the potential risks did not concern him. He writes: "That first night I had sex I didn't use protection because I thought it wasn't going to happen to me." As a result of that decision, Thomas's whole life changed, as he explains: "My girlfriend got pregnant and now I'm about to be a father."[44]

Forced to Grow Up

Thomas was only 15 years old when he found out that his girlfriend was pregnant. He was shocked at first, wondering if there was some mistake, and certainly not ready for the immense responsibilities of fatherhood. He had been a carefree guy who enjoyed shooting pool, hanging out with his friends, playing video games, and going to the movies. Once he learned that he was going to be a father, he knew that nothing would ever be the same again, as he wrote a month before the baby was due: "Sometimes I still feel strange. . . . Time has gone very fast and sometimes I still don't believe that she is pregnant. In a way, I also feel that I only have a couple of weeks left to have my childhood. I suddenly feel very old. . . . I'm only 15 and I don't even have that much money to dress myself. Imagine, now I have to go and get a better job and support not only myself, but my son and my girlfriend."[45]

> " With CDC studies showing that nearly 40 percent of teenagers do not use condoms, the implications are clear—for whatever reason, thousands of young people are putting themselves at risk for pregnancy and STD infection. "

The fear and uncertainty expressed by Thomas is typical of both teenage boys and girls once they realize they have conceived a child and decide to keep it. They have to grow up fast—very fast. When teens learn about an unexpected pregnancy, they are faced with decisions that can be painfully difficult, including whether to have an abortion, give up their babies for adoption, or continue with the pregnancy and become teen parents. In an interview published in the June 2009 issue of *Seventeen* magazine, a 17-year-old girl from New York City named Elizabeth shared her feelings about finding out she was pregnant and what she went through afterward. "The hardest thing to deal with is the way people judge me and stare now that I'm starting to show. I know what they're thinking—that I'm just a teen mom who's not going to amount to anything. I feel them doubting me, and it makes me so mad." [46]

Sobering Realities

Like Elizabeth, many teenagers decide to continue with a pregnancy, have their babies, and do the very best they can at being parents. Sadly, though, the hurdles faced by teen parents are often immense. According to the CDC, only about 50 percent of teen mothers receive a high school diploma by age 22, compared with nearly 90 percent of women who did not give birth during adolescence. A high percentage of teenage fathers also do not graduate from high school and often end up in low-paying jobs or are unable to find a job. The Yale School of Public Health explains: "Adolescent fathers typically have less educational achievement and poorer earning potential than their peers who delay parenthood." [47]

> When teens learn about an unexpected pregnancy, they are faced with decisions that can be painfully difficult, including whether to have an abortion, give their babies up for adoption, or continue with the pregnancy and become teen parents.

These and other challenges can be insurmountable for teenage parents. As a result, many end up living in poverty and having long periods of dependence on public assistance. The National Campaign to Prevent Teen and Unplanned Pregnancy states that two-thirds of families begun by a young unmarried mother are poor, and about one-fourth of teen mothers go on welfare within three years of a child's birth. The group writes: "Simply put, if more children in this country were born to parents who are ready and able to care for them, we would see a significant reduction in a host of social problems afflicting children in the United States, from school failure and crime to child abuse and neglect." [48]

Another problem faced by teen parents is a strong inheritance factor. For instance, the daughters of teen mothers are at least three times more likely to become teen mothers themselves when compared with daughters born to mothers in their twenties. According to a report released in January 2010 by researchers from Yale University, the same is true of teenage fathers and their sons. After analyzing information from nearly 1,500 males aged 19 and younger, the team found that the sons of teenage fathers were 80 percent more likely to eventually become adolescent fathers than were sons born to older men. Senior research author Trace Kershaw shares his thoughts about the study's findings: "We often neglect the importance of men in reproductive and maternal-child health. We need to recognize that men play a significant role in the health and well being of families and children."[49]

Dangerous Viruses

Health officials say that one of the most serious risks associated with teenagers having sex is the potential of being infected with one or more STDs. The most common is human papillomavirus (HPV), which collectively refers to a group of 100 or more related viruses. About 60 of these viruses cause common warts on nongenital skin, such as on the hands and feet, while the other 40 are mucosal strains. Mucosal viruses are so named because they infect the mucous membranes, which are the moist skinlike layers that line organs and cavities of the body that open to the outside.

Sheila Overton recalls one of her patients, a teenage girl who had been infected with a mucosal type of HPV that caused her to develop a particularly severe case of genital warts. Overton writes: "She came to my office with her mom because she had developed large growths in her genital area. She looked embarrassed and scared. During her exam, I found that most of Amy's genital area was covered with cauliflower-sized warts. She could barely sit down."[50] The types of HPV that cause warts, including genital warts, are considered low risk because they do not cause cancer. The high-risk types, however, are associated with several different types of cancer. In females, nearly 100 percent of cervical cancer cases result from infection with high-risk HPV, predominantly types 16 or 18. Males and females who engage in anal sex and become infected with HPV vastly increase their risk of developing cancer of the anus.

One fact that is not well known is that teenage girls are especially susceptible to being infected by HPV when they have sexual intercourse. This is because their cervixes are not yet fully developed, as Miriam Grossman writes: "The teen cervix is another way biology says wait. It's immature and vulnerable to infection due to an area called the transformation zone. The T-zone is covered by only one layer of cells, so bacteria and viruses, especially HPV, can take up residence with ease. With time, the T-zone is replaced by many layers of cells that are more difficult to penetrate."[51]

The Risks of Chlamydia

Another STD that has a high prevalence among teenagers is chlamydia, a disease that is caused by a type of bacteria known as *Chlamydia trachomatis*. One of the most common STDs, chlamydia is spread through vaginal and anal intercourse, as well as through oral sex. According to a November 2010 report by the CDC, more than 1.2 million cases of chlamydia were reported during 2009—and the group with the highest number of cases was females aged 15 to 19.

Since only about 30 percent of teens who are infected exhibit symptoms, most are never diagnosed. Chlamydia can be cured with antibiotics, but those who are not treated can develop serious health problems. In females, for instance, chlamydia infections can lead to inflammation of the cervix and/or pelvic inflammatory disease, which can cause infertility. Although it happens rarely, chlamydia can also lead to infertility in males, as well as a painful inflammation of the urethra called urethritis.

> **Health officials say that one of the most serious risks associated with teenagers having sex is the potential of being infected with one or more STDs.**

A teenager named Shellie Wolfson became infected with chlamydia because she had unprotected sex, and she has regretted that decision ever since. When she became sexually active, the possibility of pregnancy concerned her, but STD infection did not. Her assumption was that if someone was infected, she would immediately know because there would be obvious signs. So, when she met a boy who "looked totally innocent, like he'd never had sex and couldn't possibly have an STD," Wolfson did not hesitate to have unprotected sex with him. She now knows that was a huge mistake and that "looking innocent doesn't mean anything when it comes to STDs."[52]

When Wolfson developed extreme pain in her lower abdomen, she went to the doctor for a checkup. A few days later, when tests showed that she had chlamydia, she was shocked, as she explains: "After the phone call, I was in tears. Maybe I was naïve, but I really thought the pain meant I had a stomach flu. I guess I thought there was no way it could happen to me." At the time she was diagnosed, Wolfson was in a new relationship and was embarrassed to tell her boyfriend that she had an STD and that he was probably infected, too. "Really, I wish I'd just used condoms," she says. "I went through so much pain, stress and fear, and for what? A couple minutes of 'fun.'"[53]

> **Even if teenagers feel that they are ready to become sexually active, many discover afterward that they were mistaken, and they suffer because of it.**

"Emotional Bruises"

One of the consequences of teenage sex that is not widely discussed is the psychological trauma some teens go through after having sex for the first time. Even if teens feel that they are ready to become sexually active, many discover afterward that they were mistaken, and they suffer because of it. This came to light during the National Campaign to Prevent Teen and Unplanned Pregnancy's 2010 *With One Voice* survey, in which 65 percent of girls and 57 percent of boys wished they had waited longer before having sex. Other studies have shown that teens who felt pressured into sex, or acted impulsively and had sex before they were fully ready, often suffer from shame, guilt, and depression. Jennifer Ashton, a medical correspondent for CBS News, adds: "I worry about the psychological impact of sexuality and the potential for unwanted pregnancy, sexually transmitted diseases and, yes, emotional bruises."[54]

Bernadine Healy, who is the health editor for *U.S. News & World*

Report, says that teenagers who wait to have sex until they are older are less likely to suffer from depression and suicidal thoughts than those who become sexually involved at an early age. She writes: "High school abstinence is associated with better physical and mental health across socioeconomic groups, no matter how much you torture the statistics."[55] According to Healy, research has shown that teenagers who choose to remain abstinent do better in school and are more likely to attend college and graduate than those who are sexually active at a younger age.

A study that was announced in August 2010 confirmed that young people who are sexually active get lower grades and have more school-related problems than teens who abstain from sex. That was only true, however, for those who engaged in casual sex, or "hooking up" as teens often call it. Sociologists from the University of California at Davis and the University of Minnesota found that teens who were sexually active while in committed relationships did not differ from abstinent teens in their grade point average, how attached they were to school, or their college expectations. According to Marie Harvey, who is a professor of public health at Oregon State University, the study dispels the notion that all teen sex is bad. "The type of relationship really matters," she says. "When it comes to sexual behavior, it takes two to tango."[56]

No Turning Back

The consequences of teens having sex are real—and lasting. Young people may suffer from guilt and regret, find themselves to be parents years before they are ready, and/or become infected with sexually transmitted diseases. Perhaps if more teens thought about these risks and took them seriously before having sex, fewer would have to suffer because of their actions.

Primary Source Quotes*

What Are the Consequences of Teenage Sex and Pregnancy?

❝The majority of teen pregnancies in this country are unplanned, are to unmarried mothers, and are associated with serious hardship for both child and parent.❞

Katherine Suellentrop, "The Odyssey Years: Preventing Teen Pregnancy Among Older Teens," National Campaign to Prevent Teen and Unplanned Pregnancy, September 2010. www.thenationalcampaign.org.

Suellentrop is assistant director of research for the National Campaign to Prevent Teen and Unplanned Pregnancy.

❝I asked Antonia to have an abortion when I found out. I was scared. We'd only been together three months and I didn't feel ready to be a dad.❞

Ciaran Gentry, "Teenage Fathers: 'I Love My Child as Much as Any Older Dad," *Daily Mail* (London), June 26, 2009. www.dailymail.co.uk.

Gentry is a young man from the United Kingdom who was 17 when his son was born.

* Editor's Note: While the definition of a primary source can be narrowly or broadly defined, for the purposes of Compact Research, a primary source consists of: 1) results of original research presented by an organization or researcher; 2) eyewitness accounts of events, personal experience, or work experience; 3) first-person editorials offering pundits' opinions; 4) government officials presenting political plans and/or policies; 5) representatives of organizations presenting testimony or policy.

❝I have had to inform a very tearful teen that even though condoms were used when she had sex, they don't always prevent HPV.❞

Sheila Overton, *Before It's Too Late*. Bloomington, IN: iUniverse, 2010.

Overton is a physician from Los Angeles who specializes in obstetrics and gynecology.

❝I felt so disgusted with myself for wasting my virginity on someone who didn't give a damn about me.❞

Shannon T. Boodram, *Laid: Young People's Experiences with Sex in an Easy-Access Culture*. Berkeley, CA: Seal, 2009.

Boodram is an author and sex educator.

❝High teen birth rates are an important concern because teen mothers and their babies face increased risks to their health, and their opportunities to build a future are diminished.❞

March of Dimes, "Teenage Pregnancy," November 2009. www.marchofdimes.com.

The March of Dimes is dedicated to improving the health of babies by preventing birth defects, premature birth, and infant mortality.

❝In order for teens to be able to make informed choices about sex, they must truly understand the risks involved. But because of widespread misconceptions about STDs, many teens underestimate those risks, and as a result, they have sex in situations they think are safe when they in fact are not.❞

Amber Madison, *Talking Sex with Your Kids*. Avon, MA: Adams Media, 2010.

Madison is an author and public speaker who lectures teenagers and parents about the importance of safe sex.

“Teen pregnancies carry extra health risks to the mother and the baby.”

National Institutes of Health, "Teenage Pregnancy," MedLine Plus, January 5, 2011. www.nlm.nih.gov.

The National Institutes of Health is the leading medical research agency in the United States.

“It is very important to remember that most of the time you will never know if you are having sex with someone who has an STD. . . . It has nothing to do with how 'clean' someone is or how the person dresses and acts. Most people who get an STD, including HIV, do not know the person they are having sex with has one.”

Teen Source, "STDs," 2011. http://teensource.org.

Teen Source is a sexual health information website created by the California Family Health Council.

Facts and Illustrations

What Are the Consequences of Teenage Sex and Pregnancy?

- A study published in June 2010 by the Centers for Disease Control and Prevention found that **47 percent** of teenage boys would be very upset if they got a girl pregnant, and **34 percent** would be a little upset.

- According to Rachael Phelps of Planned Parenthood, **63 percent** of teenage boys and **69 percent** of teenage girls in the United States regret not waiting longer to have sex, compared with only 5 percent of boys and 12 percent of girls in the Netherlands.

- A study presented to the American Sociological Association in August 2010 found that teenagers who have **casual sex** care less about school, have lower grade point averages, and experience more problems in school than their peers who have not had sex.

- Advocates for Youth reports that only **51 percent** of teenagers who give birth graduate from high school, compared with close to **90 percent** of nonparenting teens.

- Of boys aged 15 to 18 who participated in the 2009 survey titled *That's What He Said*, **24 percent** said they would be annoyed if a girl asked them to get tested for STDs before having sex, and **11 percent** said they would refuse to do it.

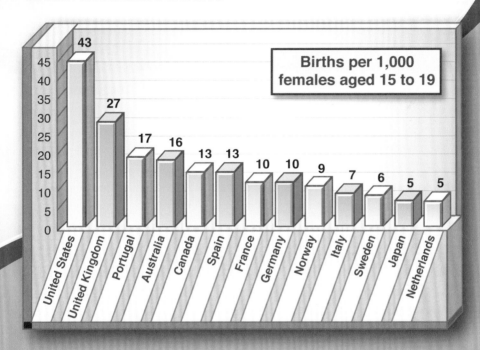

United States Leads Industrialized World in Teen Births

One of the major consequences of teenagers being sexually active is unplanned pregnancy. Although studies show that sexual activity among American teens is roughly the same as for teens in many other parts of the world, the US teen birth rate is significantly higher than in all other industrialized countries.

Births per 1,000 females aged 15 to 19

United States	United Kingdom	Portugal	Australia	Canada	Spain	France	Germany	Norway	Italy	Sweden	Japan	Netherlands
43	27	17	16	13	13	10	10	9	7	6	5	5

Source: Joyce C. Abma, Gladys M. Martinez, and Casey E. Copen, "Teenagers in the United States: Sexual Activity, Contraceptive Use, and Childbearing. National Survey of Family Growth 2006–2008," Centers for Disease Control and Prevention, June 2010. www.cdc.gov.

- NARAL Pro-Choice America states that **53 percent** of Hispanic teen girls and **51 percent** of black teen girls will become pregnant at least once before they reach the age of 20, compared with **19 percent** of non-Hispanic white teen girls.

- According to the United Kingdom's Health Protection Agency, about **10 percent** of the 15- to 24-year-olds treated for a sexually transmitted infection will be reinfected within a year.

Health Risks of STDs

Whether from inconsistent condom use, low awareness, or other factors, sexually active teens have an extremely high risk of acquiring STDs. According to the CDC, young people aged 15 to 24 represent only 25 percent of the sexually experienced population, but they acquire nearly half of all new STDs, with HPV, chlamydia, and gonorrhea being the most common among teenagers. This diagram shows the health risks.

Sexually Transmitted Disease	Health Risks
Human papillomavirus (HPV)	From vaginal or anal sex: genital warts; in females, cancers of the cervix, vagina, vulva, and anus; in males, cancers of the anus and penis. HPV spread through oral sex can cause warts in the throat, which can block the airway and cause breathing problems; cancers of the tongue, tonsils, and throat.
Chlamydia	Spread through vaginal, oral, or anal sex: in females, vaginal discharge, burning sensations when urinating, bleeding between menstrual periods, fallopian tube infection, pelvic inflammatory disease, infertility; in males, discharge from the penis, burning sensation when urinating, pain and swelling of testicles, infertility (rare).
Gonorrhea	Spread through vaginal, oral, or anal sex: in females, painful or burning sensation when urinating, vaginal discharge, bleeding between menstrual periods, pelvic inflammatory disease, chronic pelvic pain, ectopic pregnancy, infertility; in males, burning sensation when urinating and/or a white, yellow, or green discharge from the penis; painful and swollen testicles, infertility. Rectal infection in males and females can cause discharge, anal itching, soreness, bleeding, and/or painful bowel movements.

Source: Centers for Disease Control and Prevention, *Sexually Transmitted Diseases (STDs): Diseases and Related Conditions*, August 4, 2010. www.cdc.gov.

- A 2010 study by researchers from Yale University found that sons of teenage fathers were **80 percent** more likely to have a child before the age of 20, compared with the sons of older fathers.

A Slight Rise in Teen Pregnancies

After steadily declining for 15 years, the rate of teenage pregnancies in the United States increased slightly between 2005 and 2006, as did the number of births and abortions among teen girls.

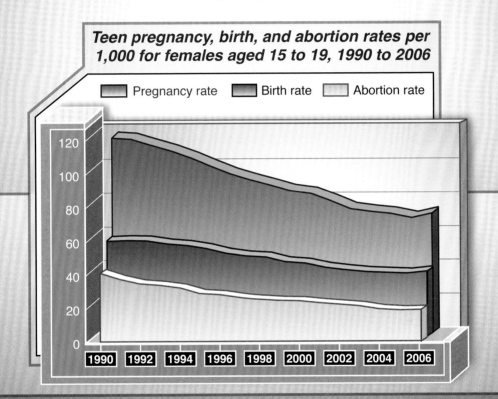

Teen pregnancy, birth, and abortion rates per 1,000 for females aged 15 to 19, 1990 to 2006

Pregnancy rate ▪ Birth rate ▫ Abortion rate

Source: Guttmacher Institute, *U.S. Teenage Pregnancies, Births and Abortions: National and State Trends by Race and Ethnicity*, January 2010. www.guttmacher.org.

- According to a 2010 report by the Guttmacher Institute, **44 percent** of black females aged 15 to 19 and **24 percent** of Hispanic females of that age group had abortions in 2005, compared with 11 percent of non-Hispanic white teens.

What Should Be Taught in Sex Education?

66Comprehensive sex-education programs work. They delay initiation of sex, reduce frequency of sex, and increase contraceptive use.99

NARAL Pro-Choice America, an advocacy group that seeks to protect women's reproductive freedom.

66Abstinence education also gives information about contraception when the schools request it, but it does not demonstrate or promote contraception. The philosophy focuses on prevention and risk avoidance, which is consistent with our message to teens about drugs, alcohol and tobacco.99

Dan Bailey, chairman of the board of the National Abstinence Education Association and executive director of the youth organization Just Say YES.

On September 30, 2010, the US Department of Health and Human Services announced that more than $100 million in pregnancy prevention grants would be awarded to states, nonprofit organizations, and school districts. In order to qualify for funding, all who sought grants were required to prove that existing programs have been effective in reducing teen pregnancy or to introduce new approaches with strong potential for achieving that goal. Altogether, 116 programs in 38 states received funding. Upon hearing the announcement, adolescent health specialist Michael Resnick shared his thoughts: "What's exciting and innovative about that is not only the full-fledged return of science to the field of teenage pregnancy prevention but also the opportunity to adapt these approaches to the needs of individual communities."[57]

Sex Ed in America

In many countries the government determines whether sex education should be taught in schools, but that is not the case in the United States. Rather, each state has the freedom to adopt its own policies on sex education. As of March 2011, 32 states and the District of Columbia required that students be educated about the human immunodeficiency virus (HIV), with the majority also mandating sex education. The remaining 18 states have no such laws in place, although school districts are free to implement their own policies. For instance, Arizona, Illinois, Michigan, and Mississippi do not mandate any type of sex education, but schools that voluntarily offer it must stress abstinence. In Colorado, which also has no legislation in place, schools that teach sex education must stress abstinence and provide instruction about contraception. The same is true in Oregon, Rhode Island, Virginia, and Washington.

Even in the absence of a federal requirement, the CDC has established criteria for comprehensive sex education programs. Of utmost importance, according to the agency, is to increase young people's knowledge of sexual issues, HIV and other STDs, and teen pregnancy, including methods of prevention. Other essential factors for teens include personal values about sex and abstinence; attitudes (pro and con) about condoms; perceptions of peer norms and sex-related behaviors; individual ability to refuse sex and limit the number of sexual partners; avoidance of places and situations that might lead to sex; and communication with parents and/or other adults about sex and contraceptives.

> " As of March 2011, 32 states and the District of Columbia required that students be educated about the human immunodeficiency virus (HIV), with the majority also mandating sex education. "

To better understand what is being taught in sex education throughout the United States, the CDC conducted a study that was published in September 2010. Based on personal interviews with nearly 2,800 teenagers from 2006 through 2008, the researchers found that 96 percent of female and 97 percent of male teens had received formal sex education before they were 18. When asked about contraception, about two-thirds of respondents said they had gotten birth control instruction by the end of high school. Of those, 52 percent of teenage boys and 46 percent of teenage girls had learned about methods of contraception while in middle school.

A Holistic Approach to Sex Ed

One sex education program that has received national attention for its effectiveness is the Adolescent Sexuality and Pregnancy Prevention Program, which was developed by Michael Carrera. As director of the National Adolescent Sexuality Training Center at the Children's Aid Society in New York City, Carrera has been working with young people for more than two decades. In the years since he developed his first after-school program, his approach has been replicated in schools throughout the United States.

> **Because abstaining from sex is, in fact, the only sure way for teens to avoid pregnancy and STD infection, many people agree that the basic concept of abstinence is a good one—as long as it is presented to young people in a way that will be effective and meaningful.**

Carrera's is a holistic program, meaning that in addition to addressing sex, sexuality, and the potential risks involved, it also helps teens focus on their personal goals and hopes for a happy, productive future. He explains: "I concluded that the way to get the sexuality message to stick was to link it with all the other things that made them whole young people."[58] Students enter the program when they are 11 years old because Carrera's experience has shown that waiting until the teenage years will likely be too late. By that time, many kids have already started having sex and/or have developed negative attitudes about sexuality that are hard to change.

Materials are age appropriate and progressively teach students about such topics as anatomy, relationships, and reproduction. The parts of the program that are unrelated to sex focus on topics such as self-image, family issues, and relationships with peers. And because research has shown that teenage pregnancies are not always accidental, young people learn about future options that may be open to them if they wait to have children. To give students a glimpse of the future, they participate in a job club where they can find work, receive a regular paycheck, and hold earnings in their own accounts. For a well-rounded approach, the program also highlights art, music, and sports.

> **When federal funding for teen pregnancy prevention was announced in 2010, states were encouraged to consider the needs of nonheterosexual students when developing sex education programs for schools.**

To evaluate the effectiveness of Carrera's sex education program, independent consultant Susan Philliber conducted a study over four years. Philliber monitored the behavior of 941 low-income teenagers aged 13 to 15 who took part in Carrera's program, along with a group of other teens who did not participate in the program. At the end of the study, 10 percent of the girls in Carrera's program had gotten pregnant compared with 22 percent in the other group. "That's more than double the percentage—and impressive,"[59] says Philliber.

Far Beyond "Just Say No"

Most people understand that the primary focus of abstinence-centered education is on teaching young people about the risks of being sexually involved and the benefits of abstaining from sex until they are older. Beyond that, however, are a number of misconceptions. National Abstinence Education Association chairman of the board Dan Bailey writes: "The problem is not in the approach but in the public's perception of the approach. Abstinence-centered education isn't focused on teaching 200 ways to say 'no.' It's about helping youths develop the life skills and abilities to successfully maneuver through a media-driven culture that bombards teens with messages telling them that teen sexual activity is fun, safe and expected."[60]

Abstinence-centered programs are often criticized for focusing too heavily on morals, thereby teaching kids that having sex is wrong. But because abstaining from sex is, in fact, the only sure way for teens to avoid pregnancy and STD infection, many people agree that the basic concept of abstinence is a good one—as long as it is presented to young people in a way that will be effective and meaningful. This was the reasoning behind a study published in February 2010 by researchers from Philadelphia and Ontario, Canada. Acknowledging the viability of the abstinence approach, they developed a program that focused on abstinence but avoided negativity and reference to moralistic aspects.

> **The STD infection rate among Dutch teenagers is markedly lower than that of American teens, and girls in the Netherlands have one of the lowest abortion rates in Europe.**

The study involved 662 African American middle schoolers from Philadelphia. The students were randomly assigned to sex education classes with one of several focuses: practicing safe sex, both delaying sex and practicing safe sex, or abstaining from sex. Students in the safe sex program were encouraged to use condoms if they had sex to reduce the risk of pregnancy and STDs. The focus of the combination program (delaying sex and safe sex) was to encourage abstinence while also providing instruction about the benefits of using condoms.

In the abstinence-centered class, all activities were designed to help students understand how an unwanted pregnancy or STD infection could potentially dash their hopes and dreams for the future. What they learned was reinforced through participation in discussions, role-playing exercises, and brainstorming sessions. Teachers were instructed not to portray sex in a negative way or to use a moralistic tone when talking with students about sex.

Upon completion of the study, the researchers monitored the students' behavior for two years and found that the abstinence-centered program was the most successful of the three. Of the students who participated in that program, just under one-third became sexually active, compared with 41 to 52 percent of those in the other programs. When the researchers made their findings public, National Campaign president Sarah Brown—who has long been an outspoken foe of abstinence-only education—had positive things to say: "This new study is game-changing. For the first time, there is strong evidence that an abstinence-only intervention can help very young teens delay sex."[61]

Sex Ed for Nonheterosexual Teens

When federal funding for teen pregnancy prevention was announced in 2010, states were encouraged to consider the needs of nonheterosexual students when developing sex education programs for schools. Doing so would ensure that gay, lesbian, bisexual, and transgender (GLBT) students would not be excluded because of their sexual orientation. Groups such as Voices for Youth and the Sexuality Information and Education Council of the United States (SIECUS) applauded this action, because GLBT students who are sexually active face many of the same risks as straight teens. If sex education classes do not take their needs into consideration, these teens may not gain crucial knowledge that could help protect them. SIECUS vice president Martha Kempner maintains that traditional sex education programs are not only designed for heterosexual students, "they are really made for a heterosexual world."[62]

The risks faced by nonheterosexual students was the subject of a study published in October 2010 that involved 17,220 New York City teenagers. The researchers found that the teens who had sex with someone of their own gender, or of both genders, were more likely to engage in risky sexual behaviors such as not using a condom. Elizabeth Saewyc, who is a researcher from British Columbia, says that nonheterosexual teens may engage in riskier sexual behavior because many sex education programs do not acknowledge gay, lesbian, or bisexual relationships. She explains: "Some teens I've seen tell me that they completely check out of sex ed because they feel what they were learning didn't apply to them."[63] According to Saewyc, sex education curriculums need to acknowledge nonheterosexual relationships so that teenagers are more likely to listen and feel comfortable discussing issues that concern them.

Yet not everyone agrees that sex education should address homosexuality, or sexual orientation at all. One of them is psychiatrist Miriam Grossman, who writes: "The primary goal of groups like SIECUS, Planned Parenthood, and Advocates for Youth is to promote sexual freedom and to rid society of its Judeo-Christian taboos and restrictions. In this worldview, almost anything goes. Each individual makes his or her sexual choices; each person decides how much risk he or she is willing to take, and no judgments are allowed."[64]

The Dutch Way

When evaluating the effectiveness of sex education programs, many experts point to the Netherlands because of its extremely low rate of 5 births per 1,000 teenage girls. The STD infection rate among Dutch teenagers is markedly lower than that of American teens, and girls in the Netherlands have one of the lowest abortion rates in Europe. Yet studies have shown that sex among Dutch teens is just as prevalent as it is among US teens, and perhaps even more so. One important difference is the Dutch approach to sex education, which is far more liberal than that of the United States.

Sexuality discussions are integrated into all levels of schooling in the Netherlands, beginning at an early age. While learning that sex is perfectly normal, kids are also taught about the importance of being responsible when they have sex, and that getting pregnant in their teens is a barrier to their future success.

Planned Parenthood's Rachael Phelps gives the Netherlands high marks for its approach to sex education. She says the Dutch philosophy is that sex is about love and commitment rather than being focused on marriage. She writes: "The Dutch see love as common, ordinary, and something teens as well as adults can expect to experience. Their corresponding expectation is that sex only occurs within a loving, committed relationship."[65] According to Phelps, this philosophy has a strong influence on teenagers in the Netherlands, where casual sex is not the norm. She cites research showing that 74 percent of Dutch teens are in a committed relationship with their sexual partner.

Parents, educators, and advocacy organizations may not always agree about what type of sex education is most appropriate and effective for teens. But what they all share in common is that they want young people to be safe and to avoid making decisions that they will someday regret.

And even those who are most passionate about their viewpoints acknowledge that no sex education program is perfect. The idea that any effort, no matter what it is, could somehow magically stop teenagers from having sex is completely unrealistic. Still, health officials hope that the number of teens who are sexually active will continue to decline, as it has over the past couple of decades. If that happens, the number of teen pregnancies and young people infected with STDs will undoubtedly be reduced as well—and that would be excellent news for the future.

Primary Source Quotes*

What Should Be Taught in Sex Education?

66There is clear evidence that abstinence-only-until-marriage programs are not effective in stopping or even delaying teen sex.99

Sexuality Information and Education Council of the United States (SIECUS) and Planned Parenthood, *Sex Education in Mississippi: Why "Just Wait" Doesn't Work*, 2010. www.siecus.org.

SIECUS provides families, educators, and policy makers access to sexuality-related information, and Planned Parenthood is a sexual and reproductive health care provider and advocate for women's health and safety.

66There is a growing body of research that confirms that abstinence-centered education decreases sexual initiation, increases abstinent behavior among sexually experienced teens, and/or decreases the number of partners among sexually experienced teens.99

National Abstinence Education Association, "Frequently Asked Questions—Correcting Misinformation in the Sex Ed Debate," 2010. www.abstinenceassociation.org.

The National Abstinence Education Association exists to serve, support, and represent individuals and organizations in the practice of abstinence education.

Bracketed quotes indicate conflicting positions.

* Editor's Note: While the definition of a primary source can be narrowly or broadly defined, for the purposes of Compact Research, a primary source consists of: 1) results of original research presented by an organization or researcher; 2) eyewitness accounts of events, personal experience, or work experience; 3) first-person editorials offering pundits' opinions; 4) government officials presenting political plans and/or policies; 5) representatives of organizations presenting testimony or policy.

Primary Source Quotes

“**In many countries, sex education is a total no go. They'd rather have no sex education than any sex education. And if there is any sex education it's only on reproduction.**”

Doortje Braeken, quoted in "Are We Taking the Pleasure Out of Sex? What a Comprehensive Sexuality Program Should Look Like," *Conscience*, Spring 2009.

Braeken is senior adviser for adolescents/youth at the International Planned Parenthood Foundation in London, England.

“**After years of Bush-administration deference to abstinence-only-until-marriage programs teen birth rates are again on the rise. . . . We should not continue funneling money into these ineffective programs.**”

NARAL Pro-Choice Virginia, "Governor McDonnell Chooses Ideology over Teen Health," August 31, 2010. http://prochoiceva.wordpress.com.

NARAL Pro-Choice Virginia is the state branch of the national NARAL Pro-Choice organization.

“**If you blame abstinence programs for a year's worth of bad news, you'd also have to give them credit for more than a decade's worth of progress.**”

Ross Douthat, "Sex Ed in Washington," *New York Times*, February 1, 2010.

Douthat is a conservative author and columnist for the *New York Times*.

“**One-size-fits-all sex ed classes will never be able to replace the advice and guidance that a parent can give.**”

Amber Madison, *Talking Sex with Your Kids*. Avon, MA: Adams Media, 2010.

Madison is an author and public speaker who lectures to teenagers and parents about the importance of safe sex.

"The real solution is for Congress to stop funding disproven programs and instead support comprehensive sexuality education that empowers students, LGBT and straight alike, to live healthy lives."

Ty Cobb, "HHS Encourages LGBT-Inclusive Sex Ed," Human Rights Campaign, August 2, 2010. www.hrcbackstory.org.

Cobb serves as legislative counsel at the Human Rights Campaign, which is the largest lesbian, gay, bisexual, and transgender civil rights organization in the United States.

"This puts the child right in the middle. The school teaches one set of values. I teach another set of values. And now the kid's stuck right at the middle."

Mikal Wilkerson, "Proposed K–12 Sex Ed Program Shocking and Outraging Parents," Fox News, July 14, 2010. www.foxnews.com.

Wilkerson is a parent who protested sex education curricula introduced by public school officials in Montana.

"You can't really subject students to an abstinence-only-until-marriage program without stigmatizing LGBT students."

Will Neville, "Prop 8 and the Future of Sex Ed," RH Reality Check, August 13, 2010. www.rhrealitycheck.org.

Neville is the director of strategic communications at Advocates for Youth.

"Some schools do not teach about sexual orientation because of objections from some religious and political groups."

American College of Obstetricians and Gynecologists, "Lesbian Teens," fact sheet, 2010. www.acog.org.

The American College of Obstetricians and Gynecologists is the United States' leading group of medical professionals providing health care for women.

What Should Be Taught in Sex Education?

- According to an April 2010 Planned Parenthood fact sheet, **90 percent** of Americans believe that sexuality education should be taught in schools, and **82 percent** support comprehensive programs that teach students about both abstinence and methods of preventing pregnancy and sexually transmitted diseases.

- In a June 2009 opinion poll by Fox News, **56 percent** of parents thought that sex education should be taught in school, **19 percent** believed that it should be left up to parents to teach, and **24 percent** thought it should be both.

- In a study of 35 sex education programs around the world, the World Health Organization found no evidence that comprehensive programs encourage **sexual activity** among teens.

- A February 2011 report by the Guttmacher Institute states that **46 percent** of teenage boys and **33 percent** of teenage girls did not receive formal instruction about contraception before they first had sex.

- According to psychiatrist Miriam Grossman, middle school–aged girls who participated in a Washington, DC, **abstinence-centered education program** were six and a half times less likely to have sex compared with their peers in other programs.

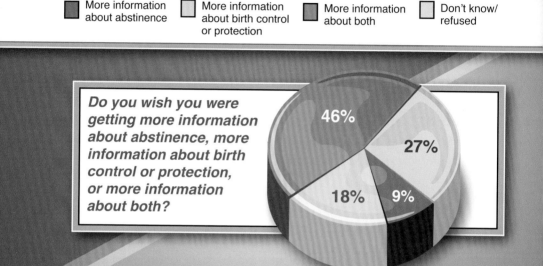

What Teens Want from Sex Education

In a 2010 survey by the National Campaign to Prevent Teen and Unplanned Pregnancy, young people aged 12 to 19 were asked what information they wanted from sex education.

- More information about abstinence
- More information about birth control or protection
- More information about both
- Don't know/ refused

Do you wish you were getting more information about abstinence, more information about birth control or protection, or more information about both?

46%

27%

18%

9%

Source: Bill Albert, *With One Voice 2010: America's Adults and Teens Sound Off About Teen Pregnancy*, National Campaign to Prevent Teen and Unplanned Pregnancy, December 2010. www.thenationalcampaign.org.

- Using data from nearly 2,800 US teens, the National Center for Health Statistics reported in September 2010 that **97 percent** of boys and **96 percent** of girls said they had received some kind of formal sex education in a school, church, community center, or somewhere else before they were 18 years old.

- A CDC report published in 2010 found that in the years 2006–2008, **52 percent** of male teens and **46 percent** of female teens received sex education on methods of birth control while they were in middle school.

When Kids Are Taught About Sex

To determine the extent to which teenagers in the United States have been educated about sex, a team of CDC researchers analyzed national survey data from 2006 to 2008 and published their report in September 2010. This graph shows how teens responded when asked about their formal sex education.

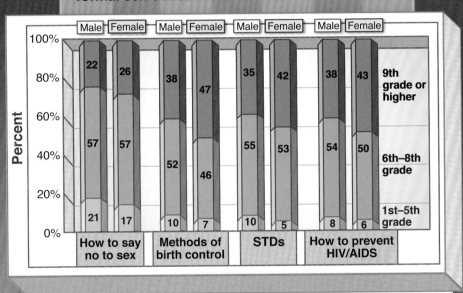

Grade when teens aged 15 to 19 first received formal sex education about . . .

Source: Gladys Martinez, Joyce Abma, and Casey Copen, "Educating Teenagers About Sex in the United States," *NCHS Data Brief*, September 2010. www.cdc.gov.

- An April 2010 Planned Parenthood fact sheet states that **63 percent** of teens aged 15 to 17 would like more information on the different methods of contraception available, **29 percent** would like more information on how to use condoms, and **59 percent** would like more information on where to go to get tested for sexually transmitted diseases.

Parental Attitudes About Sexual Orientation as Part of Sex Education

When the federal government announced its 2011 funding for teen pregnancy prevention, states seeking grants were asked to consider the needs of nonheterosexual youth in their sex education programs. This is controversial because not everyone agrees that sexual orientation should be included in sex education. To examine parental attitudes about the issue, Fox News surveyed parents in June 2009. This chart shows the responses.

At what age do you think it is appropriate to start discussing homosexuality and sexual orientation in sex education programs at school?

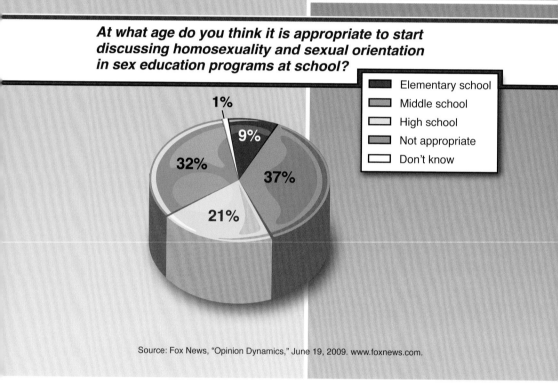

Legend:
- Elementary school
- Middle school
- High school
- Not appropriate
- Don't know

1%
9%
32%
37%
21%

Source: Fox News, "Opinion Dynamics," June 19, 2009. www.foxnews.com.

- Of the teens who participated in a 2010 survey by the National Campaign to Prevent Teen and Unplanned Pregnancy, **87 percent** said they believe it is important for teens to be given a strong message that they should wait to have sex until they are at least out of high school.

- In a CDC study published in July 2009, nearly **70 percent** of teenage girls and **66.2 percent** of teenage boys reported that they had received formal instruction on methods of birth control.

- According to an April 2010 report by Planned Parenthood, more than **three-fourths** of teens aged 15 to 17 say they need more information on birth control, HIV/AIDS, and other sexually transmitted diseases.

- In a 2010 survey by the National Campaign to Prevent Teen and Unplanned Pregnancy, **46 percent** of teenagers and **73 percent** of adults said that young people should get information about both abstinence and contraception, rather than one or the other.

- In a June 2009 opinion poll by Fox News, when asked what age teachers should start discussing pregnancy and birth control in school sex education programs, **11 percent** of parents said elementary school, **66 percent** said middle school, and **16 percent** said high school.

Key People and Advocacy Groups

Advocates for Youth: An organization that is dedicated to helping young people make informed and responsible decisions about their reproductive and sexual health.

Bill Albert: The chief program officer of the National Campaign to Prevent Teen and Unplanned Pregnancy, an organization that seeks to improve the lives and future prospects of children and families.

American College of Obstetricians and Gynecologists: The United States' leading group of medical professionals providing health care for females of all ages.

Centers for Disease Control and Prevention (CDC): An agency of the US Department of Health and Human Services that seeks to promote health and quality of life by controlling disease, injury, and disability and that compiles research on teen sex and pregnancy, as well as innumerable other health issues.

Miriam Grossman: A psychiatrist from Los Angeles who is an outspoken opponent of most sex education programs, which she says do not teach teenagers enough about the risks of sex.

Guttmacher Institute: A research organization that seeks to advance sexual and reproductive health worldwide through an interrelated program of social science research, public education, and policy analysis, and by compiling statistical reports on issues such as teenage sex and pregnancy.

Healthy Teen Network: A national organization that is focused on adolescent health and well-being with an emphasis on teen pregnancy prevention, teen pregnancy, and teen parenting.

Valerie Huber: Executive director of the National Abstinence Education Program, which is dedicated to sex education for young people that focuses on abstinence.

National Abstinence Education Association: An organization that exists to serve, support, and represent individuals and organizations in the practice of abstinence education.

National Campaign to Prevent Teen and Unplanned Pregnancy: An organization dedicated to improving the lives of families and children by preventing teen pregnancy and unplanned pregnancy among single, young adults.

Planned Parenthood Federation of America: A leading sexual and reproductive health care provider and advocate for women's health and safety and a strong supporter of comprehensive sex education for young people.

Sexuality Information and Education Council of the United States (SIECUS): An organization that provides sexuality information for young people and adults through publications, websites, training, and other resources.

Chronology

1923
The American Birth Control League, an organization dedicated to reproductive rights of females of all ages, is incorporated in New York City.

1980
According to the Centers for Disease Control, teenage pregnancies have increased more than 10 percent since 1974.

1940
The US Public Health Service specifies sexuality education as an "urgent need" in public schools and promotes this concept throughout the United States.

1920   1940   1960   1980

1942
The American Birth Control League changes its name to Planned Parenthood Federation of America.

1973
With the US Supreme Court's landmark decision on a Texas lawsuit titled *Roe v. Wade*, a woman's right to have an abortion is protected by the US Constitution. Teen girls are also afforded that right, but some states go on to pass legislation that requires parental involvement.

1955
The American Medical Association and National Education Association publish and distribute a series of informational pamphlets called "The Sex Education Series for Schools."

1978
The Adolescent Health Services and Pregnancy Prevention and Care Act is passed; it fosters the development of community-based services aimed at preventing teen pregnancy, as well as providing care to pregnant adolescents.

1981

Congress passes legislation known as the Adolescent Family Life Act, which supports programs designed to prevent teenage pregnancy by encouraging sexual abstinence.

2011

A report by the Guttmacher Institute shows that 32 US states and the District of Columbia mandate HIV education in schools, with 20 of those states also requiring sex education.

1983

German scientist Harald zur Hausen isolates the human papilloma virus type 16 from cervical cancer tumors, thus proving that cervical cancer is caused by HPV.

1996

By amending Title V of the Social Security Act, the Bill Clinton administration establishes federal funding for abstinence-only education as a strategy to reduce high rates of pregnancy and STD infection among adolescents.

1985

1995

2005

1982

The Centers for Disease Control reports that the estimated percentage of 15- to 19-year-olds with premarital sexual experience is nearly 43 percent, a significant increase from 26.8 percent in 1971.

1991

A study by the Centers for Disease Control finds that more than 54 percent of high school students have had sexual intercourse, and nearly 19 percent reported having sex with four or more persons.

2008

A Centers for Disease Control and Prevention study shows that 1 in 4 American females between the ages of 14 and 19 has a sexually transmitted disease, with HPV being the most common.

2010

The Centers for Disease Control and Prevention announces that the US teen birth rate reached 39.1 births per 1,000 girls, which is the lowest number recorded since tracking of such data began in 1940.

Related Organizations

Advocates for Youth

2000 M St. NW, Suite 750
Washington, DC 20036
phone: (202) 419-3420 • fax: (202) 419-1448
e-mail: info@advocatesforyouth.org
website: www.advocatesforyouth.org

Advocates for Youth is dedicated to helping young people make informed and responsible decisions about their reproductive and sexual health. Its website features an extensive "Topics & Issues" section as well as news releases, fact sheets, editorials, and links to blogs and podcasts.

American College of Obstetricians and Gynecologists

409 Twelfth St. SW, Suite 100
PO Box 96920
Washington, DC 20090-6920
phone: (202) 638-5577 • fax: (202) 484-1595
website: www.acog.org

The American College of Obstetricians and Gynecologists is the United States' leading group of medical professionals providing health care for women. Its website offers numerous publications, news releases, fact sheets, and a search engine that produces a number of articles about teen sex and pregnancy.

Center for Young Women's Health

333 Longwood Ave., 5th Floor
Boston, MA 02115
phone: (617) 355-2994 • fax: (617) 730-0186
website: www.youngwomenshealth.org

The Center for Young Women's Health provides education, research, and health care advocacy for teen girls and young women. Its website features information on topics related to teen sex and pregnancy, including sexual health, abstinence, contraception, and sexually transmitted diseases, and links to a "Guys' Guides" section for teenage boys.

Centers for Disease Control and Prevention (CDC)

1600 Clifton Rd.
Atlanta, GA 30333
phone: (800) 232-4636)
e-mail: cdcinfo@cdc.gov • website: www.cdc.gov

The Centers for Disease Control and Prevention seeks to promote health and quality of life by controlling disease, injury, and disability. An extensive collection of information about teen sex and pregnancy is available through its website's search engine and "A to Z Index."

Family Research Council

801 G St. NW
Washington, DC 20001
phone: (202) 393-2100 • fax: (202) 393-2134
website: www.frc.org

Through research and education, the Family Research Council promotes faith, family, and freedom in public policy and public opinion. Its website offers a variety of articles related to teen sex and pregnancy, including information about abstinence, sex education, and the importance of parents and the family.

Guttmacher Institute

125 Maiden Ln., 7th Floor
New York, NY 10038
phone: (212) 248-1111; toll-free: (800) 355-0244
fax: (212) 248-1951
e-mail: info@guttmacher.org • website: www.agi-usa.org

The Guttmacher Institute advances sexual and reproductive health through an interrelated program of social science research, public education, and policy analysis. A vast amount of information can be found on its website, including fact sheets, research reports, article abstracts, "State Policies in Brief," and news releases.

Healthy Teen Network

1501 Saint Paul St., Suite 124
Baltimore, MD 21202
phone: (410) 685-0410 • fax: (410) 685-0481
e-mail: info@healthyteennetwork.org
website: www.healthyteennetwork.org

Healthy Teen Network is a national organization focused on adolescent health and well-being with an emphasis on teen pregnancy prevention, teen pregnancy, and teen parenting. Numerous articles and fact sheets are available on its website, along with links to a number of studies.

Inspire USA Foundation

657 Mission St., #507
San Francisco, CA 94105
phone: (415) 495-4300 • fax: (415) 495-4301
website: www.inspireusafoundation.org

The mission of the Inspire USA Foundation is to help young people lead happier lives. Its REACHOUT website (which links from the main site) offers teenagers a wealth of information about all kinds of issues, with a search engine that produces numerous articles and real-life stories about teen sex and pregnancy.

National Abstinence Education Association

1701 Pennsylvania Ave. NW, Suite 300
Washington, DC 20006
phone: (202) 248-5420 • fax: (866) 935-4850
e-mail: info@thenaea.org • website: www.abstinenceassociation.org

The National Abstinence Education Association exists to serve, support, and represent individuals and organizations in the practice of abstinence education. Its website features news articles, press releases/commentary, and a "Hot Topics" section with updates on abstinence education.

National Campaign to Prevent Teen and Unplanned Pregnancy

1776 Massachusetts Ave. NW, Suite 200
Washington, DC 20036
phone: (202) 478-8500 • fax: (202) 478-8588
website: www.thenationalcampaign.org

The National Campaign to Prevent Teen and Unplanned Pregnancy is dedicated to improving lives by preventing unplanned pregnancy among teens as well as single, young adults. Its website offers national and state data on pregnancy, fact sheets, news releases, and links to numerous opinion surveys.

Planned Parenthood Federation of America

434 W. Thirty-Third St.
New York, NY 10001
phone: (212) 541-7800 • fax: (212) 245-1845
website: www.plannedparenthood.org

Planned Parenthood is a leading sexual and reproductive health care provider and advocate for women's health. The website's "Info for Teens" section provides information about sex and sexuality, myths and facts, pregnancy, and relationships. The site's "Ask the Experts" feature provides a searchable database of questions teens often ask about sex and pregnancy.

Sexuality Information and Education Council of the United States (SIECUS)

1706 R St. NW
Washington, DC 20009
phone: (202) 265-2405 • fax: (202) 462-2340
website: www.siecus.org

SIECUS provides families, educators, and policy makers access to sexuality information through publications, training, and other resources. Its website provides extensive information about teen sexuality and pregnancy, sexual orientation, sex education, reproductive health, and public policies.

For Further Research

Books

Stephen Feinstein, *Sexuality and Teens: What You Should Know About Sex, Abstinence, Birth Control, Pregnancy, and STDs*. Berkeley Heights, NJ: Enslow, 2010.

Christina Fisanick, ed., *Do Abstinence Programs Work?*, Detroit: Greenhaven, 2010.

Nikol Hasler, *Sex, a Book for Teens: An Uncensored Guide to Your Body, Sex, and Safety*. San Francisco: Zest, 2010.

Lisa Krueger, ed., *Teen Pregnancy and Parenting*. Detroit: Greenhaven, 2010.

Jeanne Warren Lindsay, *Teen Dads: Rights, Responsibilities & Joys*. Buena Park, CA: Morning Glory, 2008.

Pamela McDowell, *Straight Talk About Teen Pregnancy*. New York: Crabtree, 2011.

Heidi Williams, ed., *Teen Pregnancy*. Detroit: Greenhaven, 2010.

Periodicals

CosmoGirl!, "Should Schools Give Out Birth Control?," April 2008.

Sally Friedman, "Doctor: Teen Girls Misinformed on Body Image, Sex," *USA Today*, November 9, 2010.

Glamour, "Let's Stop the New Teenage Mom Craze," editorial, October 2009.

Cathy Gulli, "Teen Girls in Charge: When It Comes to Sex, Teen Girls Are Starting to Act More Like Boys," *Maclean's*, April 13, 2009.

Marina Khidekel, "Could Hollywood Trick You into Getting Pregnant?," *Seventeen*, May 2010.

Tamar Lewin, "After Long Decline, Teenage Pregnancy Rate Rises," *New York Times*, January 26, 2010.

Mike Males, "Behaving Like Children," *New York Times*, January 28, 2010.

Tara Parker-Pope, "The Myth of Rampant Teenage Promiscuity," *New York Times*, January 26, 2009.

Jessica Press, "The Secret Life of Pregnant Teenagers," *Seventeen*, June 2009.

Rob Stein, "Rise in Teenage Pregnancy Rate Spurs New Debate on Arresting It," *Washington Post*, January 26, 2010.

Cheryl Wetzstein, "HHS Ramps Up Funding to Fight Teen Pregnancy," *Washington Times*, October 3, 2010.

Women's Health Weekly, "Teens Are Heading in Wrong Direction: Likely to Have Sex, but Not Use Contraception," July 2, 2009.

Internet Sources

Bill Albert, *With One Voice 2010: America's Adults and Teens Sound Off About Teen Pregnancy*, National Campaign to Prevent Teen and Unplanned Pregnancy, December 2010. www.thenationalcampaign. org/resources/pdf/pubs/WOV_2010.pdf.

Miriam Grossman, "You're Teaching My Child *What*? The Truth About Sex Education," Heritage Foundation, August 9, 2010. www.heri tage.org/Research/Lecture/Youre-Teaching-My-Child-What-The-Truth-About-Sex-Education.

Kierra Johnson, "The Myth of the Teen Pregnancy Epidemic," *Huffington Post*, July 21, 2010. www.huffingtonpost.com/kierra-johnson/ the-myth-of-the-teen-preg_b_653822.html.

National Campaign to Prevent Teen and Unplanned Pregnancy, *Talking Back: What Teens Want Adults to Know About Teen Pregnancy*, 2010. www.thenationalcampaign.org/resources/pdf/pubs/Talking_Back. pdf.

————, *Thinking About Our Future: Latino Teens Speak Out About Teen Pregnancy*, 2009. www.thenationalcampaign.org/resources/pdf/pubs/ Thinking_About_Our_Future.pdf.

Rachel Sheffield, "Fewer Teen Moms but More Babies Born to Single Moms than Ever," *Foundry*, December 22, 2010. http://blog.heri tage.org/2010/12/22/fewer-teen-moms-but-more-babies-born-to-single-moms-than-ever.

Source Notes

Overview

1. Quoted in Nicole L. Fletcher, "Pregnant at 17: Rachel's Story," *Columbus Parent*, January 31, 2010. www.columbusparent.com.
2. Quoted in Fletcher, "Pregnant at 17: Rachel's Story."
3. Quoted in Fletcher, "Pregnant at 17: Rachel's Story."
4. Quoted in Ann McArthur, "A New Home for Teen Moms," *Austin (TX) Weekly News*, January 12, 2011. www.austinweeklynews.com.
5. Quoted in Mike Stobbe, "Even at Lowest, U.S. Teen Birth Rate Far Higher than W. Europe," *Huffington Post*, December 30, 2010. www.huffingtonpost.com.
6. Centers for Disease Control and Prevention, *Sexually Transmitted Disease Surveillance 2009*, November 2010. www.cdc.gov.
7. American Cancer Society, "Human Papilloma Virus (HPV), Cancer, and HPV Vaccines—Frequently Asked Questions," December 23, 2010. www.cancer.org.
8. Victor C. Strasburger, "Sexuality, Contraception, and the Media," *Pediatrics*, August 30, 2010. http://pediatrics.aappublications.org.
9. Joanna Weiss, "Students Find More Sex than Education," *Boston Globe*, December 12, 2010. www.boston.com.
10. *Seventeen* and National Campaign to Prevent Teen and Unplanned Pregnancy, *That's What He Said*, 2010. www.thenationalcampaign.org.
11. Maureen E. Lyon and Christina Breda Antoniades, *My Teen Has Had Sex: Now What Do I Do?* Beverly, MA: Fair Winds, 2009, p. 83.
12. Quoted in Erin Richards, "MPS to Discuss Providing Condoms to Students," *Milwaukee Journal Sentinel*, December 2, 2009. www.jsonline.com.
13. Lyon and Antoniades, *My Teen Has Had Sex: Now What Do I Do?*, p. 113.
14. National Abstinence Education Association, "Frequently Asked Questions—Correcting Misinformation in the Sex Ed Debate," 2010. www.abstinenceassociation.org.
15. Margaret Blythe, "Testimony Before the Committee on Oversight and Government Reform," April 23, 2008. www.aap.org.
16. Quoted in Richard Garner, "The Big Question: Why Are Teenage Pregnancy Rates So High, and What Can Be Done About It?," *Independent* (London), February 17, 2009. www.independent.co.uk.

Is Teenage Sex and Pregnancy a Serious Problem?

17. Sheila Overton, *Before It's Too Late*. Bloomington, IN: iUniverse, 2010, p. 11.
18. Quoted in Joseph Brownstein, "Bristol Palin's Cameo Role in Teen Pregnancy Trend," ABC News, January 7, 2009. http://abcnews.go.com.
19. Quoted in Rob Stein, "Teen Birth Rate Hits Record Low," *Washington Post*, December 21, 2010. http://voices.washingtonpost.com.
20. Bill Albert, *With One Voice 2010: America's Adults and Teens Sound Off About Teen Pregnancy*, National Campaign to Prevent Teen and Unplanned Pregnancy, December 2010. www.

thenationalcampaign.org.

21. Quoted in Kate Hilpern, "Teenage Fathers: 'I Love My Child as Much as Any Older Dad,'" *Daily Mail* (London), June 26, 2009. www.dailymail.co.uk.

22. Lacey McLaughlin, "Kids Having Kids," *Jackson (MS) Free Press*, November 17, 2010. www.jacksonfreepress.com.

23. Quoted in Jeanna Bryner, "Teen Birth Rates Highest in Most Religious States," MSNBC, September 16, 2009. www.msnbc.msn.com.

24. Bonnie Halpern-Felsher, *Adolescents and Oral Sex: Is It Really Something to Worry About?*, presentation at the American Association for the Advancement of Science annual meeting, February 20, 2011. http://aaas.confex.com.

25. Quoted in Rachel Rettner, "Teens View Oral Sex as Safer, but It Brings Cancer Risks," LiveScience, February 21, 2011. www.livescience.com.

26. Quoted in Rettner, "Teens View Oral Sex as Safer, but It Brings Cancer Risks."

What Influences Teenagers' Attitudes Toward Sex and Pregnancy?

27. Quoted in United Press International, "MTV Plans '16 and Pregnant' Reality Show," May 18, 2009. www.upi.com.

28. National Campaign to Prevent Teen and Unplanned Pregnancy, "Evaluating the Impact of MTV's *16 and Pregnant* on Teen Viewers' Attitudes About Teen Pregnancy," *Science Says 45*, October 2010. www.thenationalcampaign.org.

29. Quoted in Hollie McKay, "Tabloids Glamorizing Teen Pregnancy by Putting Teen Moms on Covers?," Fox News, September 10, 2010. www.foxnews.com.

30. Strasburger, "Sexuality, Contraception, and the Media."

31. Quoted in Colneth Smiley Jr., "Parents, Kids Should Be 'Enthusiastic' About Conversation," *Boston Herald*, February 13, 2011. www.bostonherald.com.

32. Laurence Steinberg and Kathryn C. Monahan, "Adolescents' Exposure to Sexy Media Does Not Hasten the Initiation of Sexual Intercourse," *Developmental Psychology*, August 2, 2010. www.temple.edu.

33. Quoted in Molly Masland, "Carnal Knowledge: The Sex Ed Debate," MSNBC, March 20, 2011. www.msnbc.msn.com.

34. Strasburger, "Sexuality, Contraception, and the Media."

35. Strasburger, "Sexuality, Contraception, and the Media."

36. Rachael Phelps, "Give the Gift of Love," slideshow, *Slate*, October 28, 2010. http://img.slate.com.

37. Amber Madison, *Talking Sex with Your Kids*. Avon, MA: Adams Media, 2010, p. xv.

38. Bill Albert, foreword to Madison, *Talking Sex with Your Kids*, p. xi.

39. Miriam Grossman, "You're Teaching My Child *What*? The Truth About Sex Education," Heritage Foundation, August 9, 2010. www.heritage.org.

40. Albert, *With One Voice 2010*.

41. Grossman, "You're Teaching My Child *What*?"

42. Russ Juskalian, "The Kids Can't Help It," *Newsweek*, December 16, 2010. www.newsweek.com.

43. Amy Bleakley, Michael Hennessy, Martin Fishbein, Harry C. Coles, and Harry Jordan, "How Sources of Sexual Information Relate to Adolescents' Beliefs About Sex," *American Journal*

of Health Behavior, January/February 2009. www.ncbi.nlm.nih.gov.

What Are the Consequences of Teenage Sex and Pregnancy?

44. Thomas C., "Life as a Teen Father-to-Be," Youth Success NYC, 2010. www.youthsuccessnyc.org.

45. Thomas C., "Life as a Teen Father-to-Be."

46. Elizabeth, in "The Secret Life of Pregnant Teenagers," *Seventeen*, June 2009, p. 127.

47. Michael Greenwood, "Teenage Fathers Often Born to Teenage Fathers, Study Finds," news release, Yale School of Public Health, January 2010. http://publichealth.yale.edu.

48. National Campaign to Prevent Teen and Unplanned Pregnancy, "Linking Teen Pregnancy Prevention to Other Critical Social Issues," *Why It Matters*, March 2010. www.thenationalcampaign.org.

49. Quoted in Greenwood, "Teenage Fathers Often Born to Teenage Fathers, Study Finds."

50. Overton, *Before It's Too Late*, p. 65.

51. Miriam Grossman, interviewed by Kathryn Lopez, "Sex Ed: Hazardous to Your Child's Health?," *National Review*, October 15, 2009. www.nationalreview.com.

52. Shellie Wolfson, "The Shock of an STD," Sex, etc., October 26, 2010. www.sexetc.org.

53. Wolfson, "The Shock of an STD."

54. Quoted in Sally Friedman, "Doctor: Teen Girls Misinformed on Body Image, Sex," *USA Today*, November 9, 2010. www.usatoday.com.

55. Bernadine Healy, "8 Traits of Teens Who Abstain from Sex," *U.S. News & World Report*, January 7, 2009. http://health.usnews.com.

56. Quoted in *Huffington Post*, "Teen Sex Not Always Bad," August 15, 2010. www.huffingtonpost.com.

What Should Be Taught in Sex Education?

57. Quoted in Rob Stein, "Obama Administration Launches a Sex-Ed Program," *Washington Post*, October 28, 2010. www.washingtonpost.com.

58. Quoted in Brenda Wilson, "Proven Sex-Ed Programs Get a Boost from Obama," NPR, June 6, 2010. www.npr.org.

59. Quoted in Wilson, "Proven Sex-Ed Programs Get a Boost from Obama."

60. Dan Bailey, "The Case for Abstinence-Centered Sex Ed," *Dallas Morning News*, April 30, 2010. www.dallasnews.com.

61. Quoted in Rob Stein, "Abstinence-Only Programs Might Work, Study Says," *Washington Post*, February 2, 2010. www.washingtonpost.com.

62. Quoted in Penny Starr, "Sex Ed Should Not Promote Only Marriage or Heterosexual Relationships, Advocates Say," CNS News, October 15, 2009. http://cnsnews.com.

63. Quoted in Zach Gottlieb, "One in Ten Teens Has Same-Sex Partners: Study," Reuters, October 25, 2010. www.reuters.com.

64. Grossman, "You're Teaching My Child *What*?"

65. Phelps, "Give the Gift of Love" slideshow.

List of Illustrations

Index

Note: Boldface page numbers indicate illustrations.

About the Author

Peggy J. Parks holds a bachelor of science degree from Aquinas College in Grand Rapids, Michigan, where she graduated magna cum laude. An author who has written more than 100 educational books for children and young adults, Parks lives in Muskegon, Michigan, a town that she says inspires her writing because of its location on the shores of Lake Michigan.